Experiences of Japanese American Women during and after World War II

Experiences of Japanese American Women during and after World War II

Living in Internment Camps and Rebuilding Life Afterwards

Precious Yamaguchi

LEXINGTON BOOKS
Lanham • Boulder • New York • London

Published by Lexington Books
An imprint of The Rowman & Littlefield Publishing Group, Inc.
4501 Forbes Boulevard, Suite 200, Lanham, Maryland 20706
www.rowman.com

Unit A, Whitacre Mews, 26-34 Stannary Street, London SE11 4AB

British Library Cataloguing in Publication Information Available

Library of Congress Cataloging-in-Publication Data Available
Yamaguchi, Precious.
Experiences of Japanese American women during and after World War II :
living in internment camps and rebuilding life afterwards / Precious Yamaguchi.
  pages cm
Includes bibliographical references and index.
ISBN 978-0-7391-9242-9 (cloth : alk. paper) — ISBN 978-0-7391-9243-6 (electronic)
1. Japanese Americans—Evacuation and relocation, 1942–1945. 2. World War,
1939–1945—Japanese Americans. 3. World War, 1939–1945—Concentration
camps—United States. 4. Japanese Americans—Social conditions. I. Title.
D769.8.A6 Y343 2014
940.53089′956073—dc23
                                                                2014038333
ISBN 978-1-4985-0863-6 (pbk : alk. paper)

Printed in the United States of America

Contents

List of Figures

Acknowledgements

The inquiries of Japanese Americans' World War II experiences began in my grandparents' home, where I listened to the word "camp" come up every now and then from my grandparents, not truly understanding what "camp" meant. Sometimes the word came up in a statement such as, "There's a camp reunion happening in Las Vegas next week, some of the people are organizing it," or "I know him, we were in the same camp together" or "Your grandpa can't eat salami, he ate so much preserved meats after getting out of camp because we were poor and it gives him allergies now." You can imagine the bewilderment and confusion I felt as a young child, trying to figure out why Grandpa ate so much preserved meat after going to camp. Does Grandma mean summer camp or camping? Eventually, my grandparents told me their stories and the "camps" they went to were nothing as I had imagined. They told very mild versions of their stories, but as I grew up and took Ethnic Studies courses in college and started to see the photographs of White business owners hanging signs saying "No Japs Allowed" or see hurtful and racist caricatures of Japanese Americans during World War II, my heart began to break because I gained a better understanding of what all four of my grandparents went through. The more I learned about the World War II Japanese American internment camps, the more I understood certain things about my grandparents such as why their work ethic was so important to them, why they are so frugal, and the reasons why it was so important for their grandchildren to receive college educations. My grandparents had once dreamt of attending college when they were teenagers, but were unable to pursue their university dreams after they were released from the internment camps because they had to work right away and support their families.

There are many individuals, organizations, and institutions I give my sincere gratitude and thanks to for their generosity while writing this book. The School of Media and Communication Studies at Bowling Green State

University played such a wonderful and important role in initiating this research. I am very fortunate to have had the support, encouragement, guidance, and inspiration from my vibrant and dedicated advisor and friend, Dr. Radhika Gajjala, and a dissertation committee composed of some of the most influential and intelligent women I know: Dr. Lynda D. Dixon, Dr. Louisa Ha, Dr. Ellen Gorsevski, and Dr. Sherlon Pack-Brown.

The kind people I have met in Ohio and at Bowling Green State University created a significant impact in my life during my time as a doctoral student and now as a professor. It is important for me to thank Dr. Lisa Chavers, Dr. Sandra Faulkner, Dr. Clayton Rosati, Dr. Michael Ogawa, Dr. Victoria Ekstrand, and Drs. Diane and Wally Pretzer. I will never forget your gracious acts of kindness and the various ways in which I have learned from you.

This book would not exist without the bravery, generosity, strength, and goodwill of the women and men who have offered their narratives, stories, life stories, information, and resources. Thank you very much Toshi Tabata, George Tabata, Michi Yamaguchi, Tomiko and Saichi Hara, Patricia Yamaguchi, June Ito, Grace Megumi, Sachi Yoshioka, Chibby Kato, Fumi Ito, Kinue Nakano, Toshi Shimoura, Toshi Kadowaki, Kathy Tashima, Soh Suzuki, Jennie Kuroyama, Mary Oi, Yoshi Matsuoka, Reiko Nimura, Jerome Joseph, Kathy Tashima, and all of the volunteers at the Japanese American National Museum, who shared so many stories and so much information with people like myself, on a daily basis.

Throughout my academic journey I have crossed paths with several people and organizations that have offered me valuable suggestions, support, and information. I extend my thanks to Dr. Kent Ono, Dr. Larry Shinagawa, Dr. Morris Young, Dr. Rory Ong, the Japanese American Citizens League – Los Angeles, the Japanese American Citizens League – Detroit, and the Japanese Consulate of Detroit. I would also like to thank Dr. Jim Brancato, Elizabeth Ortiz, Thomas Ardizzone, Micah Sadigh, Kenza Glass, Lamont Rouse, and all of my wonderful friends at Cedar Crest College who supported me during the time I was writing this book.

Most importantly, I thank my family and friends for their ongoing love and support. My love and gratitude are embedded in this text to my family and friends: Patti, David, Darrick, Sonya, Ted, and Roger Yamaguchi, Toshi and George Tabata, Michi and Tom Yamaguchi, Julie and Andy Nakano, Marci, Doug, and Paige Furuye, Andrew Lien, Drs. Linda and Eric Lien, David Tabata, Alison Tabata, Trevor and Rusty Nakano, Great Grandma Tanaka, Nydia and Armando Rivero, Sandra, Leonardo, Amanda, Amber, Cassie, and Sammie Rivero, Aaron Rivero, Israel, Bella, and Mateo Rivero, Linda Rivero, Imelda de Vera, Dianna Diaz, and all of my friends in the School of Media and Communication Studies at Bowling Green State University, especially Samara Anarbaeva and Franklin Yartey. I am blessed to have the love, humor, and support from Andres Rivero on a daily basis.

This book is dedicated to all four of my grandparents who were in the World War II Japanese American internment camps, Toshi and George Tabata, and Michi and Tom Yamaguchi, who have inspired me throughout my life. I love you all very much.

Chapter 1

Los Angeles, 1937–1942

From Cantaloupe Sunrises to the Cantaloupe Farms

She peaks through the blinds of the window to observe Los Angeles city in 1937 as the sun rises and casts a pinkish-yellow glow, as fresh as the inside of a ripe cantaloupe on the sidewalks. The morning sunlight shines through the fan-shaped leaves of a lone palm tree planted in the backyard. Boyle Heights, the Latino-populated neighborhood of Los Angeles, wakes up as hopeful and new each morning as this 12-year-old child lying on her lilac-printed bedspread. She tosses her head back onto her pillow as a newscaster on the radio in the living room announces that Japan has invaded China, but the girl listens over the radio's noise to her mother's friend at the front door of her grandparent's house.

"Have I got a man for you," says her mother's friend in a coy and delightful tone.

The young girl can hear her mother's shoe drag on the wooden floor as she shifts her hip and lets out a subtle, "Hmmm . . ." in response.

A week later, the young girl and her mother are packing up all their belongings into hard, cumbersome suitcases with weak hinges and clasps that pinch your skin if your finger gets caught between them. They make their way to Union Station where her mother pays for two one-way tickets to Brawley, California.

"Where are we going?" she asks her mother.

"Don't worry about it," her mother responds in a stoic tone. "Your father is not coming back, we're moving on without him."

She looks up at her mother, who is looking straight ahead, determined and undaunted. Her cotton dress moves back and forth as she restlessly shuffles her tiny shoes carelessly. The train arrives and they leave the City of Angels to the inland farmlands of the Imperial Valley to a miniscule-size town called Brawley.

BRAWLEY-WESTMORELAND, 1942:
"WE ALL HAVE TO LEAVE"

The young girl and her mother traded in their lives of beautiful cantaloupe-colored sunrises in Los Angeles for taking up residence on a cantaloupe farm. The mornings in Westmoreland-Brawley are hot, dry, and there are no fan-shaped palm tree leaves or sounds coming from a lively city. Instead, this weary little station town has nothing but coarse lumps of hay and farmland. There are other children the same age as the young girl living in Westmoreland-Brawley, but it is too hot to play, even for energetic 12-year-olds.

Mexican workers from across the nearby border dig, hoe, and tend the soil. Her mother is out there with them, and so is her new stepfather who is a cantaloupe farmer. He is quiet, hard working, and has a gentle smile. His fingers are rough, as if they are wrapped with the canvas used for potato sacks and his personality is warm and hearty like a savory stew slowly cooked. The only problem with him is he only knows how to make his new stepdaughter bologna sandwiches. He packs her lunch for her everyday before her bus ride to Westmoreland Elementary School.

Years pass. Mornings waiting for the Westmoreland Elementary School bus transform into mornings waiting for the Brawley Union High School bus. In 1942, the young girl who is now a teenager and a sophomore comes home from school and hears her mother screaming at her father as usual. Her mother bursts through the kitchen door, dirty from picking tomatoes, zucchini squash, and cantaloupes on their farm.

"Pack up your suitcase now," she demands. "We all have to leave." The girl's mother and father are now both inside the house scrambling, nearly flailing, to pack up as much as they can into one suitcase each.

EN ROUTE TO POSTON, ARIZONA, 1942:
"THAT IS A POOR MAN'S HABIT"

The families trudge down the dirt paths dragging their crumbling suitcases heavily like cenotaph slabs, leaving a trail of footprints large and small behind. Yelping, whimpering dogs and pets are left behind, as children cry, having to walk away from their family animals. The people are like ghosts, except much more ornery and grave in spirit, wandering through a dusty limbo toward the town's church near Brawley Union High School where several state buses waited for them. The girl and her parents ascended the stairs into the bus along with other families.

A young teenage boy stands outside as families in single-file lines board the buses toward Poston, Arizona. The image of a boy waving, almost mechanically, as the buses depart stays in the girl's mind as the stagnant landscape of Brawley and the Imperial Valley fades into the distance under a black night time curtain. She is sitting next to her father, whose legs are slightly bouncing nervously, as he thinks of all he's leaving behind.

"Hey," snaps the girl's mother to her father, "stop doing that! That's wasted energy! You know shaking your legs like that is bad luck, like shaking a tree and making all the leaves fall off! That is a poor man's habit."

Her father stops shaking his legs and the girl falls asleep, fading with the darkness and not knowing of where the bus will take her. This is the story of my grandmother and other women like my grandmother, who were evacuated from their homes into the World War II internment camps.

LISTENING TO THE STORIES OF
JAPANESE AMERICAN WOMEN

In this book I interviewed Japanese American women who were in United States World War II internment camps as well as incorporated my autoethnography of my family and I, and our story of five generations in the U.S. This research provides an opportunity to record personal narratives of Japanese American women as they tell their stories from their past experiences and their reflections. This book engages in overlapping fields within academia including communication, ethnic studies, psychology, cultural studies, Asian American studies, history, human rights, constitutional law, and political science. In the circumstance of the incarceration of Japanese Americans, the use of race and ethnicity as the justification for national segregation and unequal treatment is a clear example of how the United States has responded to its fears during World War II. Such actions on the part of those in power in the United States have succeeded in producing inequities of power that use race as a primary characteristic for discrimination (Mosher, 2002). As a feminist, intergenerational, critical, and Asian American studies project, this book looks at how unequal justice has been placed upon a group of people and how it has affected their quality of life and their relationship with future generations.

On February 19, 1942, President Franklin D. Roosevelt's Executive Order 9066 required all people of Japanese ancestry (one-eighth of Japanese blood or more) who were living on the west coast of the U.S. to be evacuated, relocated, and imprisoned into internment camps. Within this group of Japanese Americans, four of my grandparents were placed in the internment camps in Rohwer and Jerome, Arkansas, and Poston, Arizona. The story in the beginning of this chapter is a narrative my grandmother told me several times throughout my life about her evacuation experience into the internment camps. All of my grandparents were included in the 120,000 people who were forced to leave their homes, businesses, and all their belongings except for one suitcase or what they could carry, and were placed in barbed-wire camps patrolled by armed police. On December 18, 1944, in the Supreme Court the *Korematsu v. United States* case, concluded the court's decision of Executive Order 9066 as constitutional (Ball, 2001). Fred Korematsu, who had changed his name, had facial surgery to change his identity, and planned to move away from the west coast to avoid reporting to a military zone for the evacuation, was charged with failing to comply with the Military Exclusion Order. Though the case determined Executive Order 9066 was necessary during a time of war and was constitutional, the case brought attention to the Japanese American internment camp and will forever be an important case in United States and legal history. It was not until June 30, 1945, that the War Relocation Authority concluded its objectives and closed (Ball, 2001). When Japanese Americans were released from the internment camps most of them were homeless, unemployed, separated from their families, and had to start their lives over again.

There have been racist misconceptions of Japanese American people being viewed as a sick race (Daniels & Kitano, 1970) and as "aliens" in their own country (Bishop, 2000, p. 71). The *Los Angeles Times* newspaper once published the headline, "Japanese Aliens Roundup Starts," which conveyed the notion that Japanese Americans were foreign although many were actually U.S. citizens (Bishop, 2000, p. 71). This book focuses on the lives of Japanese American women who were in the World War II internment camps and how it affected and changed their lives throughout time even after they were released from the internment camps. Most of the women in this book are *Niseis* and *Sanseis* (second- and third-generation Japanese Americans) and were born in the United States. A postcolonial-turned-anti-colonial theoretical framework is used to research the ongoing effects and cultural struggles, accomplishments, and community-building Japanese American women have faced due to their experiences of the internment camps and World War II. Through ethnographic methods including autoethnography, interviews, and participant observations this research looks at the generation of Japanese American women who experienced part of their lives in the American World War II internment camps. Some of these women are the last World War II internment camp survivors and are between the ages of 70 and 95 years old. With the expansion of knowledge of different ethnic groups' experiences in the U.S., there lies hope that history can develop awareness in order to work toward the prevention of similar future shameful acts upon people such as internment camps and ethnic exclusion laws. This book highlights the narratives of Japanese American women based on their stories and testimonies.

This research project positions itself with the goals of the Second Wave of Asian American studies in relation to Communication Studies. The Second Wave is defined by the communication scholar Kent Ono (2005) as a period of questioning and challenging the first phase as well as seeking lines of power beyond the discourse of victimhood and examining nationalism through historical, social, and organizational frameworks. Ono (2005) focuses on the characteristics embedded in critical studies and rethinking the parameters of Asian American research. Furthermore, the Second Wave of Asian American studies stresses the expansion of Asian American studies as a discipline beyond the topics of immigration, acculturation, citizenship models, and national identities, commonly found in the First Wave of Asian American research, and extends on creating critical dialogue on generational, sexual, and social identities. This project moves the focus of Japanese American women who were in the World War II interment camps beyond victimhood, toward the awareness of their journeys, labor participation, and strengths of building, rebuilding, and creating successful lives for themselves and their families during times of racism, prejudice, poverty, and war.

Chapter 2

The Significance of Silence

When I was growing up in California, I would accompany my grandmother everywhere she went. She lived in a neighborhood in South Central Los Angeles and was friends with every person who lived on her block. My grandparents' neighbors were mostly all African American, and she would walk down the street and give away bags of fruits to her neighbors when her fruit trees were in season, and her neighbors were just as caring to her and my grandfather. One day she fell down on her neighbor's lawn, and her neighbor picked up my grandma in two arms like a baby and carried her into her house. Even in my twenties, I would still go grocery shopping with her and spend every weekend with her because I loved listening to my grandmother's stories, jokes, and watching her interactions with her community. She always told my mother, "If I ever need to go into a nursing home, put me in an African American nursing home," because she felt so close to her community, neighbors, and friends.

One day, when I was in my early teens, we went on an errand outside of the neighborhood to a Honda dealership where she was getting her car worked on. We waited in line at the dealership and the customer in front of us was a white male and was furious at the Honda dealership employee. My grandmother and I stood quietly in line and waited patiently pretending not to listen (even though we were listening) as the man in front of us was cussing at the employee. The angry man abruptly turned around toward us, and said to my grandmother, "Stupid JAP!!!" He stomped off, leaving my grandmother and I stunned. He was not mad at my grandmother, but I suppose since Honda is a Japanese automobile company and he turned around to see a Japanese woman, he associated her with the company in his fury.

Certain derogatory and racist words like "Jap" have a stinging sensation. It is a word that was used prior to World War II but became widely used throughout the media, in homes, and in public to describe an underlying hatred toward Japanese during and after World War II. In Uno's (2000) writing, she is called a "Jap" by some merchants while walking on her way to school and she writes, "I'm looking around. Who's a Jap? Who's a Jap? Then it dawned on me, I'm the Jap" (Uno, 2000, p. 32).

I had never even heard such a term said out loud and in person, but I knew it was an awful word. I looked at her and she appeared to be a bit startled, then I looked at him, and she said, "It's okay! It's okay!" She did not want me to say anything to him or to be angry with him. She laughed the incident off. We did not speak about it at all during out ride home.

Later that evening, when my grandfather came home from work, she told him about the incident. At first she was smiling and even laughing about it, she said, "He turned around and said, 'Stupid Jap!' to me! Haha." Then immediately after I saw her eyes tear up and her mouth frown. She almost looked like she was going to cry. Then she smiled again.

What was happening?

The details of Japanese American communication, especially in women, can be displayed in a matter of seconds. An abundance of meaningful information can be lost in seconds if one is not watching and listening closely. If an outsider was viewing this scene and had not been looking closely, she or he may not have seen the flash of a frown or the presence of tears which she never let fall. They might have just heard her laugh and seen her smile before and after she told the story and thought the incident did not hurt her at all. The context of history, culture, and identity play roles in the way we communicate. In the next chapters, I will discuss Japanese American history, culture, previous studies, and research on intergenerational communication about traumatic events.

LOCATIONS OF AN INSIDER AND OUTSIDER

I have acquired entrance into this community of Japanese American women from the time I was born since all four of my grandparents were imprisoned in the internment camps in various locations in the United States. I grew up very closely with them and observed how Japanese Americans have created supportive communities after World War II since they faced an abundance of racism, discrimination, and financial difficulties post-World War II. Many Japanese Americans who lived during World War II have put great effort into maintaining friendships and loyalties with each other for generations.

As a Japanese American, I understand some of the Japanese American communication norms such as *enryo* and *gaman*. These two Japanese words and practices express a variation of holding back, suppressing emotions, and maintaining a certain amount of politeness when communicating (especially when speaking about traumatic events or issues that can raise sadness, anger, or can threaten the balance of harmony). These Japanese norms are sometimes overlooked in some of the previous studies on Japanese Americans' communication. For example, I noticed when I would ask Japanese American women about their lives, the first response they would say was, "Oh, but my life is so boring, you don't want to hear about it," and I knew that type of response was embedded with so many layers of Japanese American communication and qualities of modesty, holding back, and sometimes shyness. As several of the Japanese American women and I continued to casually converse, and I would ask more questions about their lives and they would tell me the most interesting, inspirational, sad, or fascinating stories. There were times I felt some of the women knew they had important and urgent stories that needed to be shared, but felt it was a requirement of modesty and politeness to downplay their excitement to share some of their stories in the beginning when we were first getting to know each other. The more we got to know each other, the more they would share with me even if we were hundreds or thousands of miles away, some of the women would send me postal mail or call me.

As an ethnographer and interviewer of the same culture, I explore communicating within these norms, knowing they exist, and search for a sense of deeper information and knowledge beyond the "oh, my life is so boring response." Though I am familiar with this community and have access to its members, it does not mean I am one of them or truly understand everything they have been through because I have never been imprisoned in an internment camp nor have lived in the times of World War II. I am both an insider and outsider in this research. The women in this book are some of the last Japanese American women who hold the knowledge, first-hand experiences, and memories of the World War II internment camps.

NEGOTIATIONS OF IDENTITY AND RIGHTS OF JAPANESE AMERICANS

Japanese immigrants were the second group of Asians to come to the United States in the 1850s after the Chinese (Lee, 1999). Most of them relocated from Japan to Hawaii and then from Hawaii to the mainland of the U.S. They arrived in large numbers and the majority of them worked as laborers in plantation, industrial, and agricultural jobs in Hawaii and on the west coast of the U.S. It was not until the early 1900s that anti-Japanese American sentiments began to take place. In 1908 an agreement between Japan and the

United States took place that restricted Japanese men to immigrate into the country but accepted women into the U.S. (Lee, 1999).

In 1909 all Japanese Americans were required to join the Japan Association of America formed by the Japanese Counselor General in San Francisco, California (Gudykunst, 2001). This association controlled all the immigration

Figure 2.1   My Grandfather's Family in Los Angeles, 1910

and traveling documents from Japan to the United States. By the 1940s there were about 125,000 Japanese Americans in the U.S. and 80,000 of them had been born in the U.S. When World War II began, immigration from Japan to the United States was not permitted until the McCarren-Walter Immigration Act in 1952. Due to the previous laws forbidding Japanese men to immigrate to the U.S. in the 1950s, 86 percent of the Japanese American population consisted of women. By the year 1980, there were approximately 700,970 Japanese Americans in the United States. Only a small minority of 43,250 Japanese people were recent immigrants to the United States (Gudykunst, 2001).

The Second World War

The outbreak of World War II began on September 1,1939, when Germany invaded Poland. The war was between the Axis and Allies. The Axis included the countries Germany, Italy, Japan, Bulgaria, Romania, and Hungary. Hungary's prime minister, Gyula Gömbös, brought the three countries Hungary, Germany, and Italy together to form an alliance. Gömbös died unexpectedly in 1936, lessening the potential trilateral power of the three countries and transforming a powerful bilateral axis between Germany and Italy. Gilbert (2004) writes of World War II as, "among the most destructive conflicts in human history; more than forty-six million soldiers and civilians perished, many in the circumstances of prolonged and horrifying cruelty" (p. 1). The German invasion into Poland targeted Jewish and Polish people. On September 3, 1939, the Germans attacked Sulejow, a small Polish town of Polish and Polish-Jewish people (Gibert, 2004).

Japan entered into the Axis power through the monarchist rule of Emperor Showa. Japan gradually allied with Germany in the 1930s and provoked its first major attack against China in 1937. The Japanese military led a brutal massacre in Nanking, China, and in 1940 occupied the French Indochina Empire of Southeast Asian countries.

The British Empire, the United States of America, and the Union of Soviet Socialist Republics (USSR) led the Allies of World War II. In 1945, World War II ended with the surrender of the Japanese (Gilbert, 2004).

The Japanese American Internment Camps

On December 7, 1941, the Japanese military attacked Pearl Harbor. Two months after the attack on February 19, 1942, President Franklin Roosevelt issued Executive Order 9066 that gave the United States Army permission to exile 120,000 Japanese Americans from the west coast and relocate them into what President Roosevelt himself called, "concentration camps" (Daniels, 2002). Any Japanese American who possessed one-eighth blood of Japanese ancestry was removed from their homes and put into relocation camps in remote areas of the U.S. away from the Pacific coast. Japanese Americans left their properties, homes, businesses, were forced to abandon their pets, and fit as much of their belongings as they could into one suitcase each. They were persuaded to pack clothing for all types of weather, medications, and personal bathroom essentials all into one suitcase and many family relics and valuable objects were abandoned. On June 21, 1943, in *Koremastsu v. the United States,* the U.S. Supreme Court ruled the internment camps constitutional, due to it being a necessary action in the time of war. Though Japanese Americans in the midwest and east coast were not forced to leave their homes and belongings, many faced brutal discrimination and suspicion as anti-Japanese American sentiments took place all across the United States.

Even when Japanese Americans were released from the internment camps, they continued to feel a great need to prove their loyalty as Americans (Luther, 2003). In 1943, President Roosevelt recruited Japanese Americans into a U.S. military combat team, which contributed to the U.S. Army's 442nd regiment and the 100th battalion where Japanese Americans fought for the American side in World War II. Many Japanese Americans volunteered to join the U.S. Army to show their dedication to their American country (Luther, 2003).

On December 17, 1944, the U.S. War Department revoked the internment camps but the interned Japanese Americans had to demonstrate their loyalty by signing affirmatively on a loyalty oath questionnaire before they were released (Luther, 2003). Many Japanese Americans were eager to leave the internment camps but it was a stressful and frightening time for both young and old Japanese Americans since many of them had no homes or jobs to return to. Great challenges awaited them since most of them lost everything they had and the political climate of the country and its people still had negative feelings toward Japanese Americans. Many of the older senior citizens and adults who had children and grandchildren had a hard time leaving the camps because they had anxieties imagining how they would start their lives over again (Luther, 2003).

JAPANESE AMERICANS IN THE MEDIA DURING WORLD WAR II

The "guard dog" function of the United States media supported aspects of prejudice against Japanese American citizens. The media coverage reported about the internment camps through the U.S. government's perspective of the event, which caused Japanese Americans' versions, stories, and voices to be ignored or silenced. The "guard dog" function, researched by Donohue, Tichenor, and Olien (1995), and its relevance to Japanese American internment during World War II is the focus of Bishop's (2000) research.

According to Bishop (2000), journalists' interactions and dependence of local authorities trained journalists "to suspect potential intruders" and create awareness even if Americans did not fully understand the events taking place (p. 65). It is important to acknowledge during the time of World War II, Japanese Americans were viewed as different, threatening, and less of American citizens and even less of human beings due to their race, ethnicity, and the international conflicts taking place. The media coverage of the Japanese American internment created by journalists who took on the role of national "guard dogs" patrolled and sided with the U.S. government against Japanese Americans who were viewed as threatening (Bishop, 2000).

A clear example of how the United States has responded to its fears and contributed to the inequity of power amongst its citizens, is the incarceration of Japanese American U.S. citizens and how ethnicity was used as a justification for national segregation and unequal treatment (Mosher, 2002). Bishop (2000) applies the guard dog theory to how journalists assumed the position to "sound the alarm" to the U.S. population and communities, influenced by the political, social, and community leaders who maintained power in the U.S. during World War II (p. 65). Even when the power structures of the U.S. possessed uncertainties about their initiatives the journalists were persuaded to take on the guard dog function. Bishop (2000) wrote about ethnic groups of people, such as Japanese Americans "who lack power and influence receive little attention from 'guard dog' journalists" (p. 65). He argues, "The guard dog theory rejects the notion that the media are 'equal co-actors' in society's power structure" and journalists ended up reinforcing the views that the Japanese Americans were threatening to the U.S. (p. 67). As journalists supported the government's views and their versions of the war, Japanese Americans' voices became further silenced and distanced to the majority of the American public through the media. The news stories of Japanese Americans being rounded up and moved into the internment camps reflect different views than the actual experiences of Japanese Americans who experienced the sadness and confusion of having to leave their homes, jobs, schools, friends, pets, and the established lives they had worked so hard to achieve to move to isolated camps.

The *Los Angeles Times* used phrases alerting people on the west coast about Japanese Americans, calling California "a zone of danger" and made statements of the possibility that some Japanese Americans may be spies or saboteurs (Bishop, 2000, p. 70). The *San Francisco Chronicle* also doubted the motives of Asian American people living in San Francisco and created articles linking poverty and immigration to crime (Bishop, 2000). It is apparent these journalists missed and ignored the perspectives of Japanese Americans' experiences during this time. When the U.S. population becomes divided into ally versus enemy the proclaimed enemy becomes invisible as a person and only visible as a target or threat.

The portrayal of Japanese Americans in Bishop's (2000) textual analysis of the guard dog theory in relation to the U.S. World War II internment camps used the national newspapers: *The New York Times, San Francisco Chronicle,* and the *Los Angeles Times.* This study used the country's "most important newspapers" to display the writings on the day after the Pearl Harbor attack to the day Executive Order 9066 was issued and Japanese Americans were removed from the west coast (Bishop, 2000, p. 68). The *San Francisco Chronicle* and *The Los Angeles Times* are two extremely important newspapers because they distributed information to people on the west coast and reported what happened in their residential and nearby cities and communities. The west coast was home to many Asian Americans, especially Japanese Americans (Gudykunst, 2001).

The discrepancies of the media coverage, especially those based on the guard dog functions of the journalists and the actual lives of the Japanese American people are faced with large gaps of difference. The surveillance of Japanese Americans through the media did not portray them as victims of the internment camps caused by President Roosevelt's decision of Executive Order 9066, but portrayed internment camps as a solution toward Americans' safety. As headlined in *The Los Angeles Times,* "Japanese Aliens Roundup Starts," reflects the notion that Japanese Americans were "aliens," although they were U.S. citizens and that they could simply be rounded up like cattle, missed the larger framework of the displacement of people in the United States based upon race (Bishop, 2000, p. 71). Journalists occasionally wrote stories on Japanese American loyalty, though Bishop (2000) notices it was often contradicted with other articles on the same page reinforcing the dualistic and conflicting identities and concepts of ally or enemy. Patriotism and loyalty were often the themes of many articles. Bishop (2000) notices stories of Japanese American loyalty are often blatant and, "the average Japanese American citizen appeared in stories as a cartoon-like, flag waving caricature" (p. 75).

Contrary to mass media printed newspapers, Japanese Americans were able to create their own community publications while they were in the internment camps. The War Relocation Authority (WRA) was in charge of overseeing all the internment camp operations in the United States. According to Luther (2003), the WRA allowed Japanese Americans to establish newspapers and events within the internment camps to create characteristics of communities. These newspapers showed information about their daily lives in the internment camps although many of the writers and illustrators expressed their opinions very subtly so they would not create adverse affects amongst the American government. Within the internment camps Japanese Americans participated in national pastimes such as baseball and swing dancing (Luther, 2003).

As I read Bishop's (2000) writing on the newspaper coverage of Japanese Americans, it reminded me of how so many Japanese American women who were in the World War II internment camps told me, "I didn't want to tell my children about our experiences in camp because I didn't want them to feel ashamed or any different than other American children." It is important for Japanese American women to share their stories, but it also very understandable to see how complex and difficult it is to relive the memories they have of World War II.

THE SURVIVAL OF MEMORIES

Quantitative studies by Nagata, Trierweiler, and Talbot (1999); and Nagata and Cheng (2003) contribute important information about the effects of the internment camps after the liberation. The Commission on Wartime Relocation and Internment of Civilians (CWRIC) in 1997 redressed each interned citizen with a letter of apology and a monetary payment for the injustice served upon this ethnic group. The apology and payment represented an acknowledgement of the injustice that occurred, however the lives of the civilians who were in the internment camps were affected even after they were freed from the internment camps. In Nagata and Cheng's (2003) quantitative research on the race-related trauma Japanese Americans experienced, the researchers stated that in-depth analyses are necessary for intergenerational studies on trauma. The researchers surveyed respondents through mailback surveys and interviews, using scales to assess communication, degrees of comfort in discussing the topic of the internment camps, general attitudes about the internment camp experience, and the redress impact. Some interesting results of this study showed 3.5 percent of the participants never talked to their children about their internment camp experience and 70 percent of the internment conversations lasted 15 minutes or less (Nagata & Cheng, 2003).

In research about the long-term effects of internment camp experiences, Nagata, Trierweiler, and Talbot (1999) wrote that children of Japanese Americans who experienced the World War II internment camps relate and absorb some of their parents' low self-esteem. Through a voluntary mailback survey, the researchers compared three groups of Japanese Americans: those who were in the internment camps at a young age; those who were not in the internment camps but had parents who had experienced the camps;

and those who had not been in the camps nor had parents in the camps. The authors measured their levels of communication, ethnic socialization, outmarriage (marriage outside of their own ethnic group), general attitudes, family impact, and attitudes on the redress. Important findings included that third-generation Japanese Americans who were in the internment camps at an early age experienced differences in communication with their family than ones who were not in the internment camps and families of the interned, third-generation Japanese Americans were the least likely to have discussed the camps as central topics (Nagata, Trierweiler, & Talbot, 1999). These findings represent the discomfort and effects the internment camp has on both the people who experienced them and their future generations.

The intergenerational dialogue between Japanese American children and their parents, grandparents, and great-grandparents can give insight about the culture's stories, struggles, cultural practices, and accomplishments, which have stemmed from their experiences before, during, and after the World War II internment camps. Iwamura (2007) argues that the Japanese American World War II experience was a "defining moment in Japanese American history—one that both informs and haunts Japanese American identity, collective and individual" (p. 939). Our histories and genealogies are carried through our elders and ancestors and survive through the intergenerational communication of stories passed down from generation to generation.

There has been literature, films, and documentaries based upon the Nazi concentration and Holocaust camps and the intergenerational effects of Jewish Holocaust survivors. Research in the psychiatric field has made significant contributions to the studies of concentration camp survivors, especially with the development of the concentration camp survival syndrome and studies conducted on survivors of Nazi persecution (Barocas, 1971). The research on children and grandchildren of Holocaust survivors is still miniscule when it comes to various academic fields. Barocas (1971) states:

> Although several studies have been conducted on concentration camp survivors since the end of World War II, relatively little has been done to investigate the development of the families formed in the post-war period. One can anticipate that the damage of the concentration camp did not end with the cutting of the barbed wire or the liberation of its victims. (p. 189)

Psychiatric scholar Werner Koening (1964) found parents who were Holocaust survivors expressed their rage to their children unconsciously, without realizing it. His research showed how some of the survivors possessed aggression in which they were unable to express directly, but acted-out toward their children (Koening, 1964). The study of the emotional development of children of Holocaust survivor parents suggests different possible treatments for people who experience emotional trauma. Barocas (1971) states:

> Concentration camp survivors remain bottled up with aggressive impulses which are seemingly expressed through their children. Therefore, the process by which the concentration camp syndrome is perpetuated in the children of survivors is a highly complex and fascinating one, worthy of considerable clinical exploration. (p. 190)

Case studies have shown survivors' syndrome is transmitted across generations from survivors to their children and grandchildren. Because of this, there exist separate children and/or grandchildren-of-Holocaust-survivors syndromes (Weiss, Connell, & Siiter, 1986). The syndrome symptoms found in Holocaust survivors by researcher Solkoff (1981) includes inabilities to concentrate, mistrust of others, expression of mourning related to survivors' feelings of guilt, chronic anxiety and dread of future, chronic depression, and various other symptoms. The survivors' syndrome cannot necessarily directly be linked to the Japanese American interment camp experience since it is based upon studies that used Jewish Holocaust survivors as their sample. However, this information of how traumatic experiences have affected people throughout their lives and future generations is important in the framework of intergenerational studies on Japanese Americans who are survivors of the World War II internment camps.

As I was writing this book, I participated in several national and international conferences where I presented portions of my research. At one of the conferences I presented at in Montreal, I discussed the ways Japanese American World War II internment camp victims used silence as a way of coping and how silence is often overlooked in communication studies. After my presentation, a male audience member, who was also a professor, came up to me and gregariously introduced himself and told me he enjoyed my presentation. His smile began to weaken and his eyes became glassy, as he told me, "My father was in a Holocaust concentration camp, it really affected him and he never talked about it. He's gone now, but I can relate to the silence you speak of. I will never know what he went through or how he felt." The man's eyes began to tear up and we gave each other a handshake that turned into a hug of understanding and condolences.

In this book, when I speak of Japanese American female survivors, their identities as *survivors* are different than the survivors who suffered through the genocide and atrocities of the Jewish Holocaust. The intergenerational research on Holocaust survivors and their families has paved the way for future research focusing on many groups of people who have experienced internment camps, concentration camps, genocide, and wars. The *surviving memories* of Japanese American women who have decided to share their feelings, narratives, and histories, will contribute to the survival of our cultural identities, where we have come from, and what Japanese Americans have accomplished. Those who are still surviving are more than just the keepers of Japanese American culture, they are also the contributors to the civil rights movement, to women being in the work place, to Asian American and North American history, and creators of awareness so interment camps will never happen again to anyone in our country. Many Japanese Americans have remained silent about their experiences and previous research reflects how little they have told of their stories. Several Japanese American women and men have chosen throughout their lives to not speak about certain memories. It is easy to miss the glimpses and subtle communication of Japanese Americans. Through the stories of Native American, African American, Latina, and various ethnic and racial groups of women, memories and intergenerational communication are what contribute to the survival of our cultures.

Chapter 3

As a Child, I Did Not Know
I Was Japanese . . .

As an Adult, People Do Not Know
I'm American

As a child growing up in the diverse city of Los Angeles, I went to school with students of many races, religions, and ethnic groups. Though there was a wide range of cultures in our classroom, one would have never known it by the way we celebrated holidays such as Thanksgiving. Thanksgiving for many elementary students is the day when our teachers told us how "our" ancestors arrived to America on ships such as the Mayflower and were greeted by the Indians and natives to this new land. In our classroom we would make pilgrim hats and "Indian hats" as our teacher would call them, cut out of paper. The boys' pilgrim hats would be made out of black construction paper and formed into a geometric colonial shape resembling a cylinder. The girls' pilgrim hats would be a made of craft paper folded into a simple bonnet. The "Indian hats" were unisex, which meant according to our teacher, American Indian men and women wore the same kind of headwear, regardless and without mention of the different American Indian Nations and customs that existed and without any explanation of *why* certain headwear was worn. We cut out a band of brown construction paper and added three paper feathers to it: one red, one green, and one yellow and that signified we were Indian for the day. There we were, a bunch of young African American, Asian, Middle Eastern, Latino, and white children of all different backgrounds sitting in the classroom wearing pilgrim and Indian hats on the last day of school before the Thanksgiving Day holiday break, believing all of our ancestors came on the Mayflower and had a friendly feast with the American Indians. None of the historical tensions, relocations, or massacres of Americans Indians were mentioned on this day.

I am embarrassed to say, not only did I take part in such simplified and racist festivities in elementary school, I believed all throughout my early childhood that my ancestors landed on Plymouth Rock hundreds of years ago and that my family history was the same as the history represented in the textbooks I read in class. Like most of my classmates, our ancestors came from countries rarely mentioned in our U.S. American history books. My ancestors came in the late 1880s to America, first to Hawaii and then to California. For most of my life the people around me did not mention my family arrived from Japan several generations ago through opportunities to work as farmers, gardeners, or in factories and even one, as a mail-order bride. Why did they let me believe for so long my ancestors were pilgrims, instead of Japanese people who worked hard to obtain the American life, and were even discriminated against?

I do not remember the exact moment when I found out my ancestors did not arrive via the Mayflower, but I do remember wearing the awful paper pilgrim hat in class. At the time, it was not at all awful because I truly felt and thought I was very much an American person with the same histories as all my classmates. I believe many Japanese American people who were growing up before World War II may have felt similarly because we were born in America and are U.S. citizens. As I listen through the interview tapes of my conversations with Japanese American women, I am reminded of many of the Japanese American women who recalled having an "ordinary" childhood, playing, going to school, and having fun.

My autoethnography is part of this ethnographic research because when it comes to describing the Japanese American culture, I am part of the culture. I am a fifth generation Japanese woman, whose four grandparents were in the World War II internment camps. I have developed awareness that some of their stories have, unfortunately, not been told more to their future generations. I use my family history as just one example of a Japanese American family timeline.

As an adult I realize my mother and father have grown up and spent most of their lives not having ever directly asked their parents about the World War II internment camps. A small population of Japanese Americans represents the fifth-generation of Asians Americans like me. We are so far removed from our ancestors' stories it can be easy to believe we are just American until we are reminded through incidents or stereotypical comments such as "you speak English well," or "you must be good in math" that from our exterior appearance we are identified as Asian, not American.

After moving to the midwest in my mid-twenties, I realized no matter how Americanized I am, I was often perceived as an "international student." In my childhood, I did not know I was Japanese, and in my adulthood, people often do not know I am American. It is important for me to write about Asian American and Japanese American experiences because we are part of the American population no matter how "international" we appear to be to others. Our experiences are meaningful though the stories may have been kept silent for generations. The Japanese American population is small in numbers so we do not always have a voice that speaks as loud as some other ethnic groups who are large in numbers and unified in their causes. It is through the combined success of many ethnic and gender groups, including Native Americans, African Americans, Latinos, women, and more that have fought for civil rights that Japanese Americans too are able to participate in building an inclusive American history and future.

THE SECOND WAVE OF ASIAN AMERICAN STUDIES

Generation, gender, sexuality, and identity are some of the topics of Asian American studies research. Fifth-generation Asian Americans, like myself, are experiencing new perspectives of identity, looking forward at our future generations, and looking back at our ancestors and their experiences in the United States. As I watch my cousin have her children, I see the sixth-generation of Japanese Americans growing and watching their identities develop.

The field of Asian American studies is categorized into different waves (Ono, 2005). The first wave of Asian American research was directed toward studies on national identity and Asian American issues of political, cultural, and intellectual communities. The second wave of Asian American studies has defined itself as a period of questioning and challenging the first phase, as well as seeking lines of power beyond the discourse of victimhood and examining nationalism through historical, social, and organizational frameworks. Critical ways of rethinking the parameters of Asian American studies is the ultimate focus in Ono's (2005) writing toward drawing attention to the development of the second phase. The emergence of Japanese American women's stories in this research strives to go beyond the focus of victimhood and instead reclaim their progress and transference of culture to their future generations.

Asian American rhetoric scholar Young (2004) uses his narratives and reflections of how he grew up in Hawaii and his experiences of being a Chinese American instructor teaching in Ann Arbor, Michigan as part of his scholarship writing. Young (2004) relates his life stories and experiences of literacy into examples of rhetorical practices of cultural and national identity in various communities of the U.S. The focus on Asian Americans' abilities to speak, understand, and immerse themselves into the English language becomes a way in which they display and confirm their identities. The theme of literacy and Asian Americans' foreignness provokes a hyper-literacy importance to various ethnic groups including the author's individual experiences.

Young (2004) examines the rhetoric of Asian Americans and literacy and the assumptions and expectations of Asian Americans and the English language. For example, there are rhetorical displays of how the importance of literacy is expressed through acts such as winning a spelling bee or competitions asserting high levels of English vocabulary and literacy. The critique of the English language and the pressures Asian Americans have to master it reveals the visions of what society views as citizenship, even if the individual is of second, third, or fourth-generations. Intersections of race, ethnicity, nationalism, literacy, and American culture strive toward assimilation and stigmatize Americans who do not perform its standardizations of literacy, language, and writing (e.g., the construction of some Hawaiian students as being labeled as illiterate). This extended analysis of personal experiences and reflections are useful in research relating to rhetoric, as well as pedagogy and critical studies.

Ono (2005) uses the phrase *critical mass* to refer to the status, the quantity of contributions, and support in Asian American studies. Furthermore, it relates to a description used in physics. Ono (2005) explains what *critical mass* means in the first footnote of the book:

> I have used the term "critical mass" to pay homage to the use of the term by Asian Americanists, e.g., to the journal *Critical Mass*. By using it, I mean that there are now a significant number of people working in the field of Asian American studies, that there are many programs and some departments, that scholarship within the field is robust, that one can depend on annual conferences happening, that there are important book awards available in the field, etc. (Ono, 2005, p. 13)

Ono (2005) describes a phenomenon in time of Asian American studies experiencing an upward incline and expansion. The phrase *critical mass* relates to a philosophy founded within physics and fields outside of critical studies and communication:

> Peter X. Feng helpfully pointed out to me that the term is often used in the field of physics to mean the amount of nuclear material needed to create a chain reaction. I might also add that in organizational and business contexts, mass refers to the point at which an organization undergoes a fundamental shift in the identity as a unit resulting from a change in the way it operates. (Ono, 2005, p. 13)

The momentum and gathered mass of Asian American contributors have become a catalyst in the growth and turn of the field. The shift is identified by the scholars and contributors who have critically questioned what Asian American studies is and what its purposes are in academia, representation, identity, media, and more importantly, in communities. For Ono (2005) the field is lively, active, and ever-present with many opportunities in the interests of Asian American studies.

Literary analyses, narratives, life stories, and experiences are methods of research highlighted by Young's (2004) research and writing. The process of writing a narrative becomes the research or the study of not just one's self but of others like the writer and the people who surround, interact, and communicate with the writer. The process of reading, writing, and speaking becomes a reflective process of cultural interaction. Like Ono, Young's approach in Asian American studies takes the creation, discovery, and the act of inquiry deeper than the theoretical frameworks seen in some older intercultural communication studies. Young (2004) reveals the process of Asian Americans' reflections and their influences and tensions in communities, professional environments, and in the everyday-ness of Asian American lives.

The concept of tensions is displayed both in Ono (2005) and Young's (2004) writing about Asian Americans and communication. Much of their philosophies on the current status of Asian American studies and communication are based upon the existence of tensions within the disciplines and communities. Ono (2005) discusses the tensions involving Asian Studies versus Asian American studies, while Young (2004) emphasizes the tensions in literacy. Both authors contribute knowledge to Asian American studies. Ono (2005) takes a strong stance as an active informant within the scholarly realm, providing a mélange of various types of ethnic and gender critical research directed toward the expansion of the discipline.

Multicultural women's stories contribute to U.S. history and feminism. The reclaiming of women's experiences as an important part of U.S. history creates richness and power to different communities of ethnic women (Ruiz & Dubois, 2000). Women not only play important roles as carriers and teachers of their cultures to the future generations, they are also creators of inventions, media, science, education, and influence society. Throughout American history Japanese American women faced "severe racism and traumatic family strain, but the experiences also fostered changes in their lives" (Matsumoto, 2000, p. 478). There is a focus on difference in history between genders and amongst numerous ethnicities. Research on gender and ethnicity is expanding as well as experiences with respect to sexual orientation and social class (Ruiz & Dubois, 2000). The events and recentering of women in Asian American history is complicated, women's labor and various issues can be both liberating and oppressive, exploitative and empowering (Okihiro, 1994), which is why it is important to listen to women's narratives and *how* they are telling their stories. What may seem as oppressive to an outsider, may be empowering to the insider, and vice versa. Japanese American women's voices contribute to the growth of feminist, ethnic, and multicultural studies. They are not just keepers of culture; they were also contributors to civil rights, American history, and women in the work place during the 1940s and beyond.

Chapter 4

Examining the Crevices
In-Between Identities

When I was 18 years old and moved away to college, I wanted to learn how to cook all the delicious dishes I had tasted from home. My friends at Humboldt State University, were excited to find out I was Japanese and hoped I could cook them some authentic Japanese dishes. When I came home to Los Angeles, during the holiday season, I dug through my grandmother's stack of cookbooks. I tried to find the most worn-out looking cookbooks, because those are usually the best and showed that they had been used often. The cookbooks that had the softest pages, with the binding barely holding the pages together, and the cover almost falling off were the Japanese American ones she bought each year from Centenary United Methodist Church in downtown Los Angeles. The books usually had a group photo of Japanese Americans; one of the covers had a photo of the 442 Regiment Combat Team from World War II. The cookbook had no authors other than a long list of community members who contributed recipes, and had little or no publication information. One of the cookbooks had a "copyright pending" notation on the inside of it; these were her favorite cookbooks. These were the cookbooks my grandmother and family members used the most.

I looked inside of the cookbook to find a strange assortment of teriyaki, meatloaf, tempura, yellow cake, and Jell-o recipes. How did meatloaf, yellow cake, and Jell-o fit into this Japanese American community cookbook? It was not quite what I had in mind when I hoped to find *authentic* Japanese recipes. I inquired with my aunt about this peculiar predicament, and she said, "You have to understand, these ladies learned how to cook straight out of camp. They didn't learn how to cook Japanese dishes from their mothers when they were 15 years old, they learned how to cook American dishes for White families before they learned how to cook for themselves and their families."

My aunt was right. I thought back on how my grandparents and great-grandparents exited the internment camps and started work right away. Japanese American children who were teenagers often were separated from their parents and worked in households as domestic servants or nannies, while their parents found work in other households, factories, salons, businesses, or farms. While my grandmother was a young teenager working as a domestic servant in a Jackson, Michigan household, her father was working as a butler at a different house in the same neighborhood. I remember my grandmother telling me, "He had no idea how to be a butler or even set the table. He didn't know which side the coffee cup was supposed to go on, so he used to draw the place setting arrangement on the inside of his cuff to help him remember." In these households, young Japanese American girls who had no previous experience working and who should have been in high school, were learning how to cook mashed potatoes, roasts, and spaghetti for white families in the midwest before they learned how to cook Japanese food from their parents. These Japanese American community cookbooks represented the food we eat in our own households, a mix of Japanese, Hawaiian, American, and even traces of Italian and Mexican dishes. My childhood meals existed within the crevices of spaghetti, udon, hamburgers, and tacos, a representation of the Mexican neighborhoods my family lived in, the white household in Michigan where my grandmother first learned to cook, and my Japanese heritage.

JAPANESE AND JAPANESE AMERICAN PEOPLE IN COMMUNICATION RESEARCH

Throughout intercultural communication studies the contrast between Japanese people and American people have been used to display differences. The initial placement of Japanese people in intercultural communication studies contributes to the growth of the intercultural theoretical framework and knowledge on collectivist cultures, Asians, and Asian Americans. In Edward Hall's (1976) book *Beyond Culture,* he dedicates a chapter illustrating his experiences in Japan as a visitor and uses Japan as a contrast of how one's own culture brings new meanings when it is juxtaposed with another culture. The observations reinforce, again, the value of placing Japanese and American cultures on an opposing dualistic spectrum.

Rogers and Hart (2002) propose an important question about intercultural communication asking, "Who gains from such knowledge and who is disadvantaged?" (p. 5). The emergence of intercultural communication research from countries such as the U.S., Japan, and Korea has developed previous intercultural communication studies usually focused on the concepts of individualism, collectivism, high-context, and low-context descriptions.

The participation of global viewpoints in communication has challenged the way in which we write about culture and displayed some shifts toward critical and cultural studies (Rogers & Hart, 2002).

Orbe and Harris (2008) describe growing categories of intercultural communication research as expanding the studies of cultural differences in relation to "age, race, ethnicity, abilities, sex, nation origin, and/or religion" (p. 6). Thus, the authors write, "interracial communication, then, is typically seen as one subset of many forms of intercultural communication" (Orbe & Harris, 2008, p. 6). Characteristics of age, sex, and religion being shared all in the same intercultural paradigm can hinder the expansion of development on research specifically aimed at the issues of race (Orbe & Harris, 2008).

In intercultural research Japanese people are often used in numerous articles and research about individualist and collectivist communication styles. Research on the importance of ingroups uses Japanese individuals as an example of how students at universities strongly influence each other throughout their lives (Gudykunst & Ting-Toomey, 1988). Ingroup research using Japanese people as a representation of a collectivist culture are also found in research by Kim (1994) on the boundaries of ingroups; undifferentiated facets of collectivism using the U.S. as a model for individualism and Japan as a model for collectivism (Yuki & Brewer, 1999); measuring the degrees of collectivism between Japan, Korea, and the U.S. (Gudykunst, Yoon, & Nishida, 1987); and the levels of uncertainty avoidance in Japan (Hofstede, 1979). Yamaguchi (1994) researches the individual levels of collectivism in Japan between an individual's private-self and collective-self and Gudykunst, Gao, Nishida, et al. (1992) researches idiocentricity using Japanese and U.S. Americans as their samples. In such studies, where do Japanese Americans fit in if the study is using a sample of Japanese people and American people? These studies created between 1979 through 1999 reveal the differences of nationality more so than ethnicity and race.

In the research on language codes in relationship to kinship, the study created by Goldstein and Tamura (1975) uses Japanese grandparents, parents, and children and studies the terms of kinship expressed through siblings. The interconnectedness used in the Japanese language to display one's relationship is researched by Tamura and Lau (1992), as well as the emphasis on group identities in coherence to language, minimizing the use of pronouns such as *I* and *you,* (Goldstein & Tamura, 1975). Studies on verbalization and agreement have used Japanese language and verbalization as an example of how Asians have high ambiguity in their messages (Morsbach, 1976) and the regulation of Japanese language (Barnlund, 1975) has also been compared to North Americans in terms of assertiveness. Lim (2002) observes how the West and the East have different communication verbalization, as shown in research by Mizutani and Mizutani (1987) in how Japanese do not always say what they want and avoid precision. These examples in the article of language and verbal communication reveal the importance of context in the Japanese language. This begs the question: do these attributes also exist in Americans and/or Europeans who are of Japanese heritage? Or can such characteristics also exist in people who are of American and/or European heritage and have been born and raised in Japan? Are there generational differences in the way one's culture communicates, for example the way a Japanese immigrant who has just arrived in America, versus a fourth-generation Japanese American? These studies display the broadness of intercultural studies and research on Japanese culture. Even within a country such as Japan regional differences determine distinct cultural values, norms, and beliefs. Studies on Japanese culture have contributed to intercultural communication research but Japanese culture as a whole cannot symbolize the identities of all Asian countries and identities.

THE PERIMETERS OF POSTCOLONIAL

Moving beyond the dualist perspectives of collectivism and individualism is important in research on culture and communication. Anti-colonial theory focuses on moving beyond the perimeters, boundaries, and limitations of postcolonial theory and the studies of colonialism. Postcolonial theory is a way of understanding the effects of colonialism in cultures and the unfolding of the cultures after colonialism (Shome, 1999). Postcolonial studies on Asian, African, Latin American, and American Indian nations situate the history, location, context, and relationships through a colonial lens of analyzing the perspectives of the colonizer and the colonized, creating the need for determining the "postcolonial moment" in cultural experiences (Shome, 1999, p. 107).

Going beyond postcolonialism and the postcolonial moments should not be confined or allocated to a specific time period or generation of people. The way postcolonial theory interacts with everyday "enactments of whiteness" contribute to the normative qualities dividing postcolonial moments and the abandonment of the complex identities of people who exist within the crevices in-between the colonizer and the colonized (Shome, 1999, p. 107). Defining the moments in time in postcolonial studies derives from elements of whiteness, using the colonizer's thrust and fleeing (or sometimes defined as liberation) as the turning points of the colonized culture's changes and transformations. Determining who is affected by colonization and how they are affected derives from the embedded privilege and power of the colonizers, locating only the moments of colonization and liberation.

Japanese Americans exist in-between their heritage from Japan, and America, their home and nationality. Japanese Americans are not the only people existing in the crevices in-between the colonizer and the colonized. Throughout the country there were several individuals who were not of Japanese American heritage who acted as allies during World War II. Schmoe (1986) writes about his experiences as a faculty member at the University of Washington in Seattle and how President Sieg of the university, "issued a statement that no person at the university was under suspicion and that all students and faculty were secure in their positions" (p. 117). Schmoe (1986) recalls how he helped Japanese students relocate to various locations so they would not be interned. He writes, "we hid our 'criminal' students under a blanket in the back seat of the car on our way to the train; their only crime was that they had not been born white" (p. 117).

As an ally to Japanese Americans, Schmoe (1986) was able to experience the difficulties, sadness, and fears Japanese Americans felt during World War II. He became an advocate in helping Japanese Americans and rallied numerous churches on the west coast to help them, but found several Christian and Catholic churches remained indifferent or were not supportive of helping Japanese Americans. Schmoe (2009) writes, "an Issei woman made the statement that the Quakers were the only non-Japanese church that stood by them through the war" (p. 120). The support Japanese Americans received from non-Japanese Americans during World War II, whether it was compassionate advocates such as Floyd Schmoe who organized efforts to help those who were being evacuated and interned, or the Quaker churches, these efforts are memorable to Japanese Americans and examples of the anti-colonial framework.

Working from postcolonial theory creates groundwork to expand upon examining situated knowledge. The relationship between postmodernism and postcolonial, produce dialogues on the characteristics that contribute to modernism itself as a concept, "that posits a linear, teleological line of 'development' beginning with ancient Greece and culminating in eighteenth-century Europe ('Western Civilization')" (Krishnaswamy, 2008, p. 5). This timeline drawn upon the linear usage of locating modernity as it "represents a critical point of reference" for postcolonial studies, relies on the results of modernity as making sense of the postcolonial (Krishnaswamy, 2008, p. 5). It is critical to inquire how postmodernism and postcolonialism empowers the cultures that continually experience the various layers of colonialism and transformations throughout time? How does problematizing and destabilizing benefit and empower cultures through postcolonial frameworks if it continues to identify the people only as victimized through the actions of the colonizer? It is important to look beyond the postcolonial moments identified on a linear timeline and look beyond what the colonizer sees as their points of liberation. It is important to analyze how the person changed their victimization into strength, empowerment, and new opportunities. The events we use to indicate apparent changes in the culture cannot be based or defined through limited moments of colonialism or the successes or failures of modernism, but the ongoing power, privilege, and contextual negotiations that are always transforming.

POSTCOLONIAL TURNED ANTI-COLONIAL THEORETICAL FRAMEWORK

Japanese Americans being imprisoned in internment camps during World War II is researched here through an anti-colonial framework. The concepts of the history, context, knowledge, nationality, and power play major roles in the Japanese American internment camp experience. The work of Gandhi (2006) on postcolonialism-turned-anti-colonialism builds upon Foucault's (1984) various concepts of technologies, genealogies, contextualizing and historicizing issues in relation to power and knowledge. Gandhi (2006) stresses Foucault's argument of research and the uncovering of knowledge about genealogies will run "up against its own desire to postulate a competing and self-defeating enthronement or 'majorization' or 'minor' thought systems" (p. 182). When we observe history from a superficial level, utopianism seems possible through the dualistic lens of ally and enemy. Yet, when we take a closer look at the technologies interwoven in historical issues, the postcolonial lens becomes blurred as cultures overlap and intertwine, such as those of Japanese Americans. This population of people of Japanese ancestry and also American were imprisoned by their own nation. One cannot divide this identity between one or the other because the Japanese American identity is both composed and influenced by characteristics from both nations. A contributing factor in the anti-colonial framework is to acknowledge "a growing awareness of the interconnectedness between diasporic domestic and foreign causes," and this relates to Japanese Americans as they are culturally interwoven through multiple identities (Gandhi, 2006, p. 123).

Foucault's (1984) ideas of knowledge and power are referred to as *technologies*. Technologies are the joining of power and knowledge resulting in "the objectification of the body" (Rabinow, 1984, p. 17). The ideas of technologies relating to the Japanese American World War II experience are twofold: first, the technologies that were used to confine and segregate a group of American citizens were based on their ethnicity, blood quantum, and fear; and second, the technologies of the U.S. government during World War II affected the relationships and lives of the people who were once imprisoned even after they were freed from the internment camps. The act of relocating people from their homes and taking away everything they own including their jobs, education, pets, and opportunities, and placing them in desolate locations in the United States is an act of taking away their knowledge and power as a citizen, and placing them under the power of the nation that is imprisoning them. The knowledge and power used against Japanese American interned citizens was an institutional tactic to docile the bodies and affected the interned prisoners for years and generations beyond the actual internment experience. There are various influences of power and knowledge in a time of war and they have the ability to create disciplinary control in time and space, to the point where the prefix of *post-* in postcolonialism becomes indefinite because it continues to influence the identities and relationships of the present and future.

Similar to the beliefs of Foucault's distrust in universal truths (1984), Foucault's ideas of historicizing the context of history follows similar goals of the second wave of Asian American studies. The U.S.'s prejudicial acts of imprisoning all people who possess one-eighth or more Japanese blood and who were living on the west coast does not only address the status of citizenship as "deviant or exotic" (Ruiz & Dubois, 2000, p. xi) but it also examines this event as an important piece of U.S. history and how the wrongful act of imprisoning a whole ethnic group was produced by a set of technologies. As Rabinow states (1984), "For Foucault, there is no external position of certainty, no universal understanding that is beyond history and society" (p. 4).

Foucault's philosophies of historicizing the power and knowledge used to manipulate individuals, create docile bodies, confine, and punish condemned bodies produces a rich awareness of diverse issues relating to various ethnic groups' statuses, beliefs, and cultures in the present. The way Japanese Americans in the World War II internment camps were imprisoned reflects a type of "punishment as a complex social function" (Foucault, 1984, p. 171). Feelings of "shame, frustration, and bitterness," of their civil rights were enforced by being imprisoned and the loss of everything they owned (Matsumoto, 2000, p. 485). The attempt to dominate the body, in terms of the Japanese American World War II internment experiences did not end after they were released from the barbed-wire fences, but their identities were changed after they were imprisoned; shamed and segregated from society. The postcolonial moment in this event should not be recognized as the moment when Japanese Americans were released from the internment camps because they continued to struggle against many of the American people who still viewed them as enemies. It is also important to argue, that not all Americans hated Japanese Americans, which is why the anti-colonial framework of Gandhi (2006) is suitable for the study of Japanese Americans.

Foucault's process in examining issues based upon their traceable histories and place within societies inspires a philosophical approach to the communication between the interned generation and their future generations. It is necessary to identify the roles of power and knowledge in this study and to keep in mind its relation of the second wave of Asian American studies and underlining caution against universal truths. In relation to Asian American studies, this examination goes beyond identifying the U.S.'s act of segregation and imprisonment as wrong. Its goal is to question how technologies were used against those who were imprisoned and how technologies can now be used to empower the Japanese American women and their children and grandchildren with a new sense of knowledge and power about their cultural identities. Women who were once imprisoned by the U.S. government can use the knowledge and power of their experiences to educate their future generations about their culture and the struggles the United States once used against them.

Krishnaswamy (2008) believes imperialism minimizes "the possibilities of representation of the subaltern within the state apparatus, and to suppress the very possibilities of dissent" (p. 13). The use of postcolonial theory and the issue of Japanese American internment camp survivors must go beyond binary ways of thinking of separating the Japanese identity from the American identity. Gandhi (2006) produces philosophies on anti-colonial thought that surpass the creations of binarist perspectives of postcolonialism. The postcolonial theoretical framework is not sufficient in looking at Japanese American's World War II experiences because postcolonialism indicates the *post* status of colonialism when many events of colonialism, such as internment camps, have significant lingering colonial effects on the culture or group of people throughout their future generations. Japanese Americans existed in the crevice of the in-between and interconnectedness of embracing both characteristics from U.S. and Japanese cultures. Postcolonial theory often disregards the in-between-ness of other possibilities of colonialism and disruptive events that transform identities throughout history that bleed into the present, and the future.

Chapter 5

From Issei to Gosei

Ethnography and Autoethnography of Generations

In this ethnographic research I use my own family history as an example of the Japanese American generations and communities in the United States. This study is not only about my family; it is about Japanese American families. I am a fifth-generation Japanese American woman whose family experienced the World War II internment camps and I have personal experience on the cultural norms, relationships, interactions, and generational differences. Not all Japanese Americans have the same exact experiences and stories as my family and I, which is why I base most of this research on the narratives and stories of several Japanese American women outside of my family. However, many Japanese Americans, especially of the *Gosei* generation (fifth generation), may find similarities to my family's stories.

In order to establish a history of my family's immigration I show a chronological timeline of my mother's side of the family because there is more information on the exact years and locations known than on my father's side. In the beginning of the 1890s my great-grandfather's (my mother's mother's father) parents immigrated from Japan to Maui, Hawaii. His parents were the first generation of Japanese Americans to come to the United States. In Japanese language the word *Issei* describes the first generation of people to come to the country. Sometimes other cultures and individuals may consider the first generation of their family to be the first person who is *born* in the U.S, but in Japanese and Japanese American history, Issei usually describes the first generation of the family to *arrive* in the United States.

Growing up in a city like Los Angeles where there were many different ethnic groups and generations of Asian Americans, I remember the acronym "F.O.B." or "fob" was often used in junior high school and high school, which stood for "fresh off the boat." I often times found while growing up,

Figure 5.1   A Family of Four Generations of Japanese American Women

it was important for my Asian American friends to not "dress like a fob" or "act like a fob," especially if they were of the first or second generation Asian Americans.

When my great-great-grandfather and great-great-grandmother arrived to Maui, Hawaii in the early 1890s they were literally fresh off the boat, a boat ride that lasted a little over 16 days. A few years after they immigrated my great-grandfather was born in 1896 in Hawaii. In this research we will call him "Gio." Gio is not his name but is a sort of child-like Japanese nickname used. The word Gio comes from the word *Ogi-san*, which means grandfather in Japanese and this is what my mother, uncle, and most of the family called him.

Like my great-grandfather, Gio, my great-grandmother was also born in Hawaii. In this research we will call her Bayo, which is also not her real name, but a Japanese nickname given to her by her family. The word *Oba-san*, means grandmother in Japanese. The exact year Bayo's family arrived to Hawaii from Japan is unknown, but it is speculated it was around the same time my great-grandfather, Gio's, family arrived.

My great-grandmother, Bayo, was born in 1904 in Hawaii. During her birth, there was no official documentation or record made of her birth so when she visited Japan as an adult, she possessed no official documentation of her birth or U.S. citizenship. Therefore, in order to visit Japan she first had to take a U.S. citizenship exam even though she was born in the United States, so she could obtain official citizenship documents so she would be able to come back to the U.S. after her trip to Japan. Gio and Bayo moved to California after Bayo returned back from Japan (date currently unknown).

Gio and Bayo had their first and only child in 1925, my grandmother Toshi (my mother's mother). My grandmother married my grandfather, who was born in 1926, and gave birth to their son, my uncle, in 1953. A year later she gave birth to my mother in 1954. My father was born in 1947 and his family moved out to Los Angeles when he was a child and he grew up in the same neighborhood as my mother. Both of my parents grew up in South Central, Los Angeles. The region had a small population of Japanese Americans and many people of my grandparents' generations came to live in this area after the World War II internment camps. In order to gain a better sense of the neighborhood and the context of my grandparents and parents' lives I interviewed my mother about growing up in the area.

After World War II several Japanese Americans created communities in Los Angeles neighborhoods and its surrounding areas. South Central Los Angeles was home to numerous Japanese Americans and their families after they moved back to California from the internment camps. "The Crenshaw area" as my parents called it, also known as Leimert Park, was in South Central Los Angeles, and composed of Japanese American and African American residents. This neighborhood is where communication, culture, and race take place. Kurashige (2008) writes about the ethnic relationships in neighborhoods where Japanese Americans lived after World War II. He states Japanese Americans living in southern California, "were welcome in southern California so long as they confined themselves to the proper social and geographical place defined by whites" (Kurashige, 2008, p. 23).

Several Japanese Americans who were in the World War II internment camps lived in the Crenshaw area and in Baldwin Hills. Through ethnographic methods, I immersed myself in the lives of many of the women I interviewed and was able to speak with their family members, husbands, children, grandchildren, friends, and neighbors. One of the women I spoke to was also my mother. Patricia, was 52 years old when I interviewed her, and had a lot of memories of the Crenshaw area in the 1950s and 1960s. Communication within the Japanese American community in the Crenshaw area was developed with their own authentic characteristics, integrating Japanese words with English. This way of speaking Japanese is informal and would not be acceptable in Japan or in a formal Japanese setting. Patricia explains:

I remember Japanese Americans speaking their own English language. Most words were English, but they would add a 'no' before a noun, maybe in place of 'the.' It made it sound more Japanese, even though they were speaking English. Sometimes they would throw in a Japanese adjective because it was a better description, for example 'gocha, gocha', describing a little boy's constant energy. They would always say there was no English word for it.

Even within the Japanese American community, there were divisions and borders in the Crenshaw area. The street Crenshaw Boulevard was described as a dividing line between some of the Japanese American South Central communities. Though this account of memories about the Crenshaw area focuses on post-World War II experiences, Japanese Americans resided in this neighborhood before, but mostly after World War II. The Leimert Park sub-neighborhood was the center of the Crenshaw district and "was a symbol of white privilege during the interwar era—a time when racial animus accumulated and patterns of racial oppression consolidated in Los Angeles" (Kurashige, 2008, p. 34).

The decades following post-World War II marked some of the most violent and racially charged events in the United States, especially in urban areas such as South Central. Neighborhoods in Los Angeles were always changing, and the population of people and their cultures continued to do so in many urban areas. The Martin Luther King Jr. assassination was a catalyst to sparking the flame of all the racial tension in Los Angeles during the 1960s. Patricia explains how one day when she was walking home from junior high school with one of her White male friends, he was "jumped" by a group of African American teenagers and was beat up very badly. After that incident, he and his family left the neighborhood and Patricia never saw him again. The combination of rising unemployment rates, racial tension, and a period of "swift racial transition" (Kurashige, 2008, p. 268) contributed to the "White flight" (p. 269) that occurred in South Central Los Angeles.

Walking down the street in the Crenshaw area, when grandmother Toshi was alive, I would see her wave to her African American and Black neighbors, as some of the children and adults gave her hugs. One of her neighbors recently asked my grandfather what my grandmother Toshi's birthday was because he wanted to get it tattooed on his arm because she made such an impact on his life as he was growing up. Almost a quarter of the Japanese American women interviewed in this book, live or once lived in the Crenshaw area, where businesses such as the Holiday Bowl bowling alley and Crenshaw Square were hangouts for the people like my parents, the children of the Japanese American Niseis and Sanseis who were in the World War II internment camps. Although two of my grandparents have passed away, my grandmother Michi, on my father's side, and my grandfather George, on my mother's side, still live in the Crenshaw area and remain closely tied with their community.

In 1980, my parents gave birth to a set of twins, my twin sister and I. During childbirth, my twin sister died and my mother, who was having a difficult childbirth, thought I might die too. Fortunately, I survived and my father named me Precious Vida, meaning Precious Life (*vida* translates into *life* in Spanish). In 1985 my parents welcomed my younger brother, and in 2007, my father unexpectedly passed away. My grandmother (my mother's mother) passed away the following year and thus the cycle of life, death, and the passing of generations takes its course showing how little time we have to gather information about each of our family member's life experiences.

My autoethnography is only a portion of this research about Japanese American women who were in the World War II internment camps. I interviewed 16 individuals who grew up in California during their childhood and identified English as their first language. Most of the Japanese American women I interviewed came from middle-class families who owned small business such as markets, restaurants, beer parlors, and hotels. Some of the Japanese American families owned farms and produce stands. Some Japanese Americans worked at stores, hotels, and a variety of jobs before World War II. Most of these women are not from the same family as each other, though their lives were similar in that they grew up around the Los Angeles area and lived the simple American lifestyles most children and teenagers lived during that time of going to school, participating in social activities, and doing chores around the house.

ETHNOGRAPHY THROUGH THE GENERATIONS

After over eight years of creating this research and writing this book, I have been able to develop different relationships with the Japanese American women who were in the World War II internment camps. Toward the end of writing this book, I had found out two of the women I had interviewed passed away a couple years ago, and two more women recently have developed Alzheimer's disease several years after I last interviewed them. Their memories, stories, and experiences are embedded in this book through our interviews. Having loved ones and people around us pass away is part of this ethnography's focus on the stories people choose to share and keep silent throughout their lives. The passing away of a person's life along with their memories displays the inevitability of an individual's boundaries in time, space, and communication.

Terhi Rantanen (2005) designed the ethnographic study in her book *Media and Globalization* focusing on the concepts and dimensions of time, space, participants, mediated communication, generation, and globalization. The limitations of conceptual definitions and methodologies should not be a reason to force researchers to work within the boundaries of established epistemic frameworks but to extend the knowledge and possibilities outward. Rantanen's (2005) research includes ethnographic case studies of three families of four generations, in which she calls a "multi-sitedness" research location (p. 14).

This book looks at a moment in history and how it affected Japanese American women through ethnographic methods. I have gained information and insight on how Japanese Americans women faced challenges with their cultural identity, the socio-economic difficulties after they were released from the internment camps, the racism they experienced in American society, and how their experiences have been told to their children and grandchildren. Like Ratanen's (2005) research, this project includes concepts of globalization, communication, generations, history, locations, time, and spaces.

Similar to Ratanen's (2005) research on four generations of three families, many of the Japanese American women who were in the World War II internment camps also discuss their past and future, families, and generations. For example, it was likely for the Japanese American women in this book to voluntarily discuss their parents and grandparents' generation as well as their children and grandchildren's generations. Some of them were even able to share a bit of information about their great-grandparents' generation or their great-grandchildren's generation, which would create perspectives of fifth and sixth generations of their family. Women have the power to possess information about several generations of people and can be located at the center of many of future generations' cultural practices.

How is this type of research currently limited by the boundaries and current frameworks of intergenerational research? The intergenerational model comes from the family sciences discipline (Pollack, 2004) and strives to show how characteristics that are practiced in one generation within a family, such as violence for example, can be passed down to the next generation within the family. The choice to use this model with the research of Japanese Americans, who have been in internment camps and how their experiences affected the lives of their children and grandchildren, could be appropriate if one were to apply it along with a quantitative method, since the model uses statistical analyses to find significance. Since the intergenerational model displays the transmittal of traits or practices from one generation or another, it cannot be used with methods other than coherent linear quantitative methods.

The combination of intergenerational research paired with ethnographic methods is complex. Ethnography is a method that strives to search for an understanding of human cultures through the participation of gaining membership in a culture (Spradley, 1979). Membership in a culture guides the individual's behavior and defines her or his point of view as an attempt to provide entry into the observed culture, phenomenon, or event (Heider, 1976).

The recollection and memories of Japanese American women who were in the World War II internment camps transcends time; it uses one's memory as an account of occurrences and a source of information. Though the Japanese American women are obviously no longer in the internment camps or at the locations, they are recalling a sequence of events in their own personal lives in which they have to remember a setting and how that setting affected them based upon their surviving memory. The authenticity of their memories is what serves the continual transformation and growth of their identities.

THE POSSIBILITIES OF MICROAGGRESSIONS DURING THE INTERVIEW PROCESS

The microaggressions of Japanese American women who were in the World War II internment camps can be multidimensional. The microaggressions of Japanese American women can be racially, ethnically, nationally, and gender-related and influenced. In order to gain an understanding of Japanese American women who were in the World War II internment camps and the microaggressions they may have faced during their interned process, it is important to understand a bit about the ways in which Japanese American women in general may deal with aggressions due to their cultural upbringing and norms.

The challenges Japanese American women who were in the World War II camps have faced throughout their lives are the issues of being treated as second-class citizens and the inequities of power as American citizens. Many of the Japanese Americans imprisoned in internment camps were second- and third generation American citizens whose ancestors came to the United States in the 1850s (Gudykunst, 2001). A surprised expression or comment from an interviewer of a Japanese American's ability to speak English fluently is an example of a microaggression that may take place. Doubts of citizenship and ability to immerse one's self into the American culture are constant issues of Asian Americans in general. Sue and Sue (2008) identify microaggressions toward Asian Americans in the form of questions and statements such as, "Where are you from?" and "You speak English well" (p. 114). These microaggressions can translate into the message, "You are not American," which is hurtful to Japanese Americans who were in the World War II camps and all the struggles they have had to face after the camps (Sue & Sue, 2008, p. 114). Sue and Sue (2008) acknowledge, "The forced internment of Japanese Americans are social realties" (p. 90). Statements doubting a

Japanese American's commitment to their country such as, "that is unusual your brother fought on the U.S. side during World War II" can be identified as a microaggression because many Japanese Americans dedicated their lives to fighting for the United States as their country.

The psychological impacts of microaggressions can be detrimental to the research process and to the interviewee's well-being. Cook (1990) emphasizes the multidimensional gender constructs related to the psychological issues of women and men. Cook (1990) states, "Psychological sex differences are more subtle and complicated than they first appear" (p. 371). This statement may be true especially with Japanese American women since the American cultural process of gender socialization often conflicts with various aspects of Japanese gender socialization. The two conflicting socialization processes combined with the difficult times of World War II makes the issue of identifying and analyzing the psychological impacts of microaggressions even more important and critical.

When World War II began, immigration from Japan to the United States was not permitted and immigration from Japan did not take place again until the McCarren-Walter Immigration Act in 1952. Due to the previous laws forbidding Japanese men to immigrate to the United States in the early 1950s 86 percent of the Japanese American population consisted of women (Gudykunst, 2001). The U.S. American political system created a change in the familial relationships of Japanese Americans since the majority of the population was made up of women and laws restricted male family members from immigrating to the United States. Microaggressions regarding statements of passiveness toward Japanese American males such as fathers, grandfathers, uncles, brothers, or friends can create negative views in relation to the counseling process as the manifestation of certain stereotypes (Constantine, 2007). The functions of Japanese American male influences were purposefully and politically minimized by the United States to lessen the impact Japanese American males could make in society and the political and financial power they could possess. The inequity of political and national power often creates the image of the Asian American male as being absent or passive. Cook (1990) writes, "This individualistic view of sex differences is that each sex is predisposed to experience certain psychological problems as a result of gender socialization" (p. 371). What makes this gender predicament even more culturally intricate is Japanese heritage derives from values in which individuals have the duty to bring pride to their families and communities. The diminished power of Japanese American men in the United States affected the visibility of Japanese American males in the United States. Because there were fewer Japanese men in the United States due to immigration laws, Japanese women had to take on more responsibilities and create strong bonds to support their families and communities.

Interviewing Japanese American women can take more time than expected because of the Japanese American communication styles influenced by the Japanese communication values of modesty, harmony, and holding back. Though many Japanese Americans have adopted many aspects of American cultural norms, the tendency to possess embedded Japanese communication norms is apparent, especially for women. According to Ivey and Ivey (1999) interviewing, "may be considered the most basic process used for information gathering, problem solving, and information and advice giving" (p. 12). Interviewing Asians and Asian American people can turn this "basic process" into a much more complicated process due to Asian communication norms. A case study in Ivey and Ivey's (1999) book by Weijun Zhang talks about the difficulty in counseling a particular Chinese man. The author states, "When Chinese people see the need to express disagreement, they usually take great care not to hurt the other's feelings or cause another to lose face" (p. 200). This concern of disrupting harmony or losing face is similarly applicable to the Japanese culture as well. A Japanese or Japanese American person may be answering questions in a polite manner so as to not create emotional or environment turbulence.

AWARENESS OF *ENRYO* AND *GAMAN* IN JAPANESE AMERICAN COMMUNICATION

The ingrained communication styles to *enryo* and *gaman* are difficult to define in the English language; there is no one word that describes the values and defines the natural acts of these words in a communication context. They are both words meaning to suppress emotions and are displayed often. If the interviewer gains understanding of *enryo* and *gaman*, she or he will realize Japanese Americans place an emphasis and deep value on the concepts of modesty or not wanting to express anger or sadness. In order to research aspects of Japanese Americans communicating their stories and life experiences it is important to know characteristics of their culture that derive from Buddhism and common Japanese beliefs, such as the concepts of *enryo* and *gaman*. A Japanese American woman may choose not to express emotional feelings *not* only because of concepts such as *gaman* or *enryo*, but because she may feel as if others do not understand the context and history of her identities and stories in the first place. Nagata and Cheng (2003) refer to these inherited communication styles of Japanese Americans. *Enryo* expresses the way in which a person practices self-restraint and *gaman* describes the way in which Japanese Americans suppress their emotions, both concepts are used to maintain harmonious effects in communication and go beyond face-saving strategies (Nagata & Cheng, 2003). These cultural practices of restraint can make the interviewer's job difficult because if the interviewer asks a difficult question a Japanese American person may try to answer the question in an unbiased and vague way, especially if she or he feels like the interviewer has no or little knowledge and understanding of their history and/or culture.

The act of remembering and recalling World War II can be a very stressful situation. Ivey and Ivey (1999) emphasize relaxation or creating a relaxed environment as a directive strategy for the interview process. The strategy of getting an Asian American person to relax in order to tell their story is an effective approach. Some interactions with a Japanese family such as drinking tea, eating, and having leisurely discussions are techniques used to create a relaxing and harmonious environment.

Sue et al. (2008) also states, "Because many racial microaggressions are usually unconscious, perpetrators are unlikely to be aware of the true motivation behind their actions" (p. 278). This awareness is crucial in the interview process of Japanese Americans. Many of the women face dual and overlapping identities of cultural norms. The more recent generations of children and grandchildren, the third, fourth, and fifth generations, may have little knowledge about their histories and identities because their parents or grandparents were too ashamed to tell them. The act of interviewing Japanese Americans is not an easy task but without the knowledge of microaggressions and an understanding of their culture the process can be very threatening to the interviewee's mental health.

THE ADAPTIVE INTERVIEW PROCESS

This study uses ethnographic methods, including informant interviews with Japanese American women who were in the internment camps. Yin (2003) stated that one of the most important sources of information in a qualitative study comes from an interview. Lindloff and Taylor (2002) concluded the best informants are ones who have had experience in the culture, are well-respected by their peers, served in the scene in many different roles, and are knowledgeable about the local language and context. Ethnography helps to give insight and information on cultures through the participation of membership in cultures (Spradley, 1979).

The Japanese American women who experienced the internment camps are the epistemic community embodied with the knowledge of the internment camps and possess the first-hand experiences. Ethnographic notes and interviews were gathered for this research. Japanese American women were selected through individual contacts (such as my grandmothers), referrals from family, friends, and members of the Japanese American Citizens League in Cleveland, Detroit, and Los Angeles. Throughout time each woman began to refer other individuals with the characteristics of being a Japanese American woman who has experienced the World War II internment camps to me. I gathered 16 interviews from Japanese Americans 70 to 95 years old that experienced the World War II internment camps and were living in California, Nevada, Ohio, or Michigan. The interviewees were asked open-ended questions face-to-face which were recorded with a tape recorder and then transcribed.

After having read studies about Japanese Americans who were in the World War II internment camps and how their interviews were guided by a list of questions in very formulated and academic settings, I realized how important it is to adapt to the interviewee's comfort zone and environment in order to experience a deeper meaning of communication. The person being interviewed may feel most at ease in various informal settings such as their house or dance studio. The adaptive interview process takes into consideration the individual's characteristics rather than just the researcher's needs. For example, some interviews that took place in this research were in the women's homes. Other interviews took place in public places and one interview even took place after the interviewee and I danced together in her jin shin jitsu studio. The process of adapting to a person's individual needs and her comfort zones, includes but is not limited to her age, ethnicity or ethnicities, generation, gender, sexuality, socio-economic background, religion, the region where she lives, occupation, hobbies, life experiences, preferences, and more. The adaptive interview process transforms and adapts the ethnographer's questions and interests into ongoing conversations in hopes to bring more information about the individual's life experiences, personality, and insights to the surface. I did not see myself as limited to a set of questions, hourly time limits, or environments for ethnographic moments to take place.

Accompanying and accepting invitations from some of the individual interviewees to various events were helpful in exploring the ethnographic sites and communities. In this research, the ethnographer is both an insider and an outsider. I view myself as an insider because I understand much of the context, culture, and the cultural relationships within the Japanese American community because I am Japanese American and have grown up closely with Japanese Americans who were in the World War II internment camps. I will also always be an outsider too, because of my generational status, age, location, and personal experiences. I never experienced growing up during World War II, lived in an internment camp, nor had to face the challenges Japanese Americans had to overcome post-World War II. I am not part of the community who helped other Japanese Americans baby sit each other's children when they went to work, helped one another find jobs, or understood what it felt like to be evacuated out of my home and relocated to a desolate internment camp. It is important for me to express and understand the boundaries of where I will always stand as an outsider.

Chapter 6

Growing Up During World War II

Evacuation, Internment, and Labor

In this book I use direct quotes from the Japanese American women I interviewed to anchor their stories as the focus of the research. Seeing the exact words they used to describe events and feelings is important to this research. As shown in the previous chapter, where I described my grandmother on my mother's side of the family, tell my grandfather how a man called her a "Stupid Jap!" and laughs when she says it though her eyes become watery is significant in seeing the juxtaposition of words, actions, and expressions used to express feelings in Japanese American communication, especially of the Nisei and Sansei generations after World War II. Several of these women have overlapping histories and share common stories and feelings as each other, especially in regards to the evacuation for Executive Order 9066.

After the Japanese military bombed Pearl Harbor, Japanese Americans that lived on the west coast were forced to evacuate their homes and were imprisoned into internment camps in states such as Colorado, Arizona, Wyoming, Texas, Idaho, Montana, Arkansas, and Utah. The Executive Order 9066 affected their ownership of homes, businesses, education, and relationships. Monica Sone (1995), in the book entitled, *Nisei Daughter,* depicts her experiences of the Executive Order 9066 evacuation in Seattle. She first published her book in 1952, only a little over a decade after Japanese Americans had entered into the internment camps.

Almost all of the women I interviewed felt the American lives their parents and grandparents built for them was very pleasant and seemed to understand the sacrifices their parents made for them in order to create stable lives. The transition from their daily lives as U.S. citizens changed when Executive Order 9066 forced Japanese Americans on the west coast out of their homes, as Toshi T, who was living in Brawley, California, during the time of the evacuation stated:

> When we were evacuated, we were only allowed to take one suitcase. I was just a little girl at the time, so I stuffed as much clothes as I could into the suitcase. At the train station, the hinges on my suitcase broke and all my clothes spilled out everywhere. I started to cry, but my father stayed very calm and helped me with my clothes. Everything around me seemed so chaotic and I was scared.

Most Japanese Americans on the west coast were allowed to take only one suitcase each or what they could carry and had to leave additional belongings behind, including major financial investments such as their cars, houses, pets, and businesses. Community leaders, academics, businessmen, and teachers of Japanese arts traditional or martial arts were the first to be arrested (Wakida, 2000). Japanese Americans worked so hard to establish homes, businesses, friendships, and educational opportunities for their children and had to abandon it all. This traumatic experience contributed in external and internal changes in their individual identities. Pets were also left behind, as Fumi I. remembers:

> We were evacuated into camp when I was 11 years old. Before the evacuation, my parents owned a hotel and beer parlor in downtown Los Angeles, which they worked very hard to get and establish. They had to leave their whole business, house, and lives that they made behind. We even had to give our dog to our neighbor.

During the World War II evacuation, Japanese Americans had no idea where they were going to be relocated to and how long they would be imprisoned. There was little time to find storage units or places to put their belongings. My grandmother and her family, who were living in Brawley, California, remembers her father running to all of the Japanese American houses and telling them to pack up as much stuff as they could and store it in their barns since they lived on farmland and everyone had their own barn. It was important for them take only what was truly essential and valuable to them, such as warm clothing, shoes, and medications. Women who were pregnant and the elderly had to also enter the interment camps, no exceptions were made.

Japanese Americans experienced life in different relocation internment camps in Arizona, Wyoming, inland California, Idaho, Utah, Arkansas, Montana, and Colorado. The majority of women in this study were evacuated from their homes in southern California and relocated to the Santa Anita horse racetrack, California, where their families were forced to stay in horse stables. Kinue recalls:

> First we were put into the Santa Anita racetracks. We stayed in the stables. Straw mattresses. We had to stuff them with straw and the smell and the stench of the

horses, and the urine, and all that junk. And then from there we were sent to Arkansas; the bayou. Of course they set up these camps in very desolate areas.

Santa Anita racetrack was a place two of my grandparents were evacuated to before they and their families were assigned to relocation camps eastward in Arkansas. From the Santa Anita assembly center, Japanese Americans were then relocated to different internment camps throughout the midwest. They traveled by bus and train to desolate areas where they were put behind barbed wire and kept as prisoners in their own country. My grandmother on my father's side of the family said:

> The first camp I went to was Santa Anita, the assembly center, and we lived in the horses' stalls (laughs) which had a really nice aroma (laughs). We all took showers together where they had the services for the horses. Ohhh, doesn't that sound exciting? And we all ate at the mess halls and we were teenagers then, right? So we didn't have school at that time and we all kind of worked on the camouflage nets, you know, that they were using for the war, and actually, we were just teenagers during that time.

From the Santa Anita assembly center, my grandmother, Michi, was sent to the Rohwer, Arkansas, internment camp. As shown in the description above, my grandmother, used brief moments of laughter to relieve a bit of the uneasiness in the conversation as well as display the absurdity that she and so many Japanese Americans being forced to live in the horse stalls and shower together where the horses showered. She is a lady who grew up well-mannered, taking Japanese music lessons, and with an understanding of etiquette from both Japanese and American cultures and traditions. I remember she and I were having a relaxed conversation and interview at the time at her house. However, when I listen to our conversation on the interview tapes I realize there are moments in the interview when she would talk about difficult times and also laugh as a way of lightening up the sad topics and easing up the tension. Most likely, she and I may not have even realized her reaction of laughing when she was telling the story.

I find myself as a Japanese American woman, displaying similar reactions when I am telling a difficult story or participating in an uncomfortable conversation too. It is not so much a laughter that represents humor nor does it indicate she is not taking the interview seriously, but it a way of transforming a somber topic into something much lighter and easier to discuss, and to put the other person at ease in a certain way. I have known my grandmother for over 30 years and through different struggles with her health, losing people she has loved, I have never seen her cry. She is one of the most social people I've ever met and through her gregarious and gracious personality, I know she is a woman of so much strength.

LIFE INSIDE THE INTERNMENT CAMPS

On December 7, 1941, the Japanese military attacked Pearl Harbor. Two months after the attack on February 19, 1942, President Franklin Roosevelt issued Executive Order 9066 that gave the United States Army permission to exile Japanese Americans from the west coast and relocate them into internment camps. Any Japanese American living on the west coast, who possessed one-eighth blood of Japanese ancestry was put into relocation camps in remote areas of the United States away from the Pacific coast. They were kept unaware by the government about how long their stay in the camp would be and if they would ever be released from the internment camp.

Yoshi: Working in the Poston Internment Camps

Yoshi, a Japanese American woman, and her family were forced to leave beautiful Oceanside, California, and she and her family were relocated to Poston, Arizona. Her memories include the following details:

> I remember when we left Oceanside by train and then we had to take a bus to Poston, by the time we got there and signed in, it was already dark. When I think about that, I don't know how we ever got to our little room. There was no lighting. We were out in the beaten sun, in the desert, so we had to carry our luggage, and 18 is an age where I would say, you knew what was going on but didn't really understand the circumstances. When we first went to camp, we were all looking for some kind of work in the camp. A lot of us worked in the canteen or mess hall with my friends. Of course we hated that job and then we eventually went to different kinds of jobs. I started working for the hospital as a nurse's aide. Camp life was pretty miserable. But I guess we learned to appreciate the hardship.

Like several of the Japanese American women interviewed in this book, the women would say similar statements similar to Yoshi's proclamation, "Camp life was pretty miserable. But I guess we learned to appreciate the hardship." The women would state an honest truth about their challenges and struggles, but then follow it with a positive statement. If I were to have interviewed them several decades ago, I wonder how they would have told their stories? Would they still have stated a negative truth, followed by a positive statement? Sometimes, it would be the opposite pattern, where a positive statement was made, followed by a negative, such as, "Camp wasn't so bad. But it really hurt me to see that my country did not see me as an American." This reflects a common display of how the Japanese Americans, both women and men, who I interviewed spoke about their experiences.

Japanese American families tried to stay together in the camps and create communities and activities in the internment camps such as classrooms, baseball teams, dance classes, and music performances. They lived in barracks and weather-proofed their living conditions when it snowed in the winters or became blistering hot in the summers. Together, Japanese Americans united as communities to keep each other safe, active, comfortable, and healthy.

Toshi K.: A Journey of Heartbreak and Entrepreneurship

The Japanese American people inside the internment camps tried to help each other and build communities within the internment camps. Many of the internment camps had makeshift schools and clinics. Toshi K., who is the eldest Japanese American woman I interviewed and in her 90's lived in Toledo, Ohio. Between the time I interviewed her and now as I write this book, I was sad to have found that she has passed away. Before entering into the internment camp, she was already married and had a baby daughter. While she was in the internment camp, she was scheduled to give birth to her first son. She remembers a traumatic experience in the Poston, Arizona camp:

> I remember in camp, I lost a baby boy. (Face saddens, eyes get teary). The doctor, I will never forgive him, but he was a young doctor. In delivery, I lost my baby boy in the internment camp.

Toshi K. remembers this experience as one of the saddest moments in her life in the internment camp. She remained strong and faced numerous challenges while in Poston. While in the internment camp, she also worked as a hairdresser. She had graduated from beauty school before entering Poston and had worked at a salon in Little Tokyo, Los Angeles (Japanese town). The owner of the beauty salon that she worked at was also in the Poston internment camp. Through her skills she found a sense of empowerment and a way to keep herself busy while in the internment camp. She recalled, "He [the owner of the beauty salon] had some equipment, but the resources were all very primitive. We would give perms for $5." Toshi K. was able to use her skills and her talents to make some money while in the internment camp and was also able to get a job quite quickly at a beauty salon and eventually became the owner of Toshi's Beauty Salon in Cleveland, Ohio, after she left Poston, Arizona. She worked very hard throughout her life at the beauty salon where she had a talent for coloring women's hair and then used that talent to tint eyeglass lenses at Toledo Optical Laboratory, Inc., where her husband was the chairman. During her interview, she spoke with pride on her accomplishments and the successful lives she and her husband built together in Ohio.

Chibby: From Exploitation to Ownership

Before World War II, many Japanese American families were dedicated to fulfilling their dreams and ambitions in the U.S. and wanted to be successful. Like several ethnic groups throughout U.S. history, Japanese Americans also believed in the American dream and worked hard to acquire it. Chibby, a second-generation Nissei woman was born in 1928 in Los Angeles. Her parents came from Fukui, Japan, when her father was 42 years old and her mother was only 18 years old. They had met in Japan through an arranged marriage.

Chibby's mother was one of the two first-generation Issei women to have a sewing school in Los Angeles. In the early 1900s Chibby's mother taught sewing and tailoring to high school and college girls in Southern California and her father was a farmer. In 1912 a terrible frost killed several farmers' crops in Southern California. During this decade Japanese Americans worked in the agricultural industry and made up 85 percent of the population in the sugar-beet industry (Molina, 2006, p. 45). Fortunately, because her father's farm was located in a valley, the frost did not affect his farm and he was able to make $10,000 that season, which was a lot of money during that time. He gave away all the money he earned that season to the other farmers and families in the area. Being a farmer in California was no longer a stable job for a Japanese American citizen. With campaigns and slogans exhibiting peoples' distaste for Japanese Americans and the agricultural jobs they had taken, the slogan such as "Keep California White" was used in the 1920s (Molina, 2005, p. 45). Chibby said:

> He was really a saint. Because of that, my mother suffered (financially) and she decided she would have a career of her own so she started to take the horse and buggy and went to Sacramento. They were on the outskirts of Sacramento (Elk Grove) and she went to sewing school. The next season, she decided to move back down to Los Angeles, with or without my father (laughs), and so she came down here and he followed her and he became a janitor at Bullocks department store. He was one of the night crew of all Japanese people.

After Chibby's mother graduated from sewing school, she opened up her own sewing school in Los Angeles. Later, she bought a hotel with 20 rooms and ran her own hotel and business. While interviewing Chibby, I realized how her family has been composed of truly strong and hardworking women. She tells me when she was a child, her sister who was only 12 years old at the time, would drive them to their Sunday school across the city and they never missed a day of class in five years. She did not have a license at that age but her parents were so busy it was the only option they had for transportation. Chibby and her family tried to avoid getting relocated into the internment camps but they were unsuccessful:

We moved to Sacramento because one of our relatives said they would not have to go to camp, and we got up there and then six weeks later we had to evacuate to the internment camps. So we went to Fresno Assembly Center and from there we were sent to Jerome, Arkansas, and then the Jerome, Arkansas camp closed and then we were sent to . . . well we had four choices, it was either Amache, Heart Mountain, Rowher, or Hila, and Hila was our last choice and my father was quite elderly and we thought maybe we could go to Colorado because my uncle used to live there. But anyway, we ended up in Hila (laughs).

Chibby went to school in the internment camp. During her time in the internment camp, it was the first time she ever had a Japanese American girl friend because most of her friends prior to when she entered the internment camp were of different ethnicities and races other than Japanese American. Through the internment camp, she met a lot of different people and participated in Japanese American cultural events. I felt one of the most interesting aspects of her story was the consistency of the strength she and the women in her family possessed.

In 1945 Chibby left the internment camp to finish high school. While she was in the Hila internment camp she came across a post seeking a Japanese American girl to work in a domestic position for a young couple who worked in Hollywood. She took the train from the Hila internment camp to Hollywood and lived with the young couple while attending Hollywood High School. She felt lonely without her sister and parents and remembers during this time some people in Los Angeles would not even speak to her because she was Japanese American. Working as a high school student and a domestic house worker was difficult. Chibby said:

They made me work quite hard. They didn't wake up until noon and I was just getting home from school at noon and I was like a full-time maid. I was young and the thing that would bother me was when she would give me her dirty personal laundry, but other than that it was ok because of the learning experience. Then after I graduated I realized I shouldn't stay there because she had a baby and it was not even a week old and she would go out to dinner or something and would leave the baby with me. To me it was a challenge because I didn't know what to do at that young age, but then again, like everything else when I finally had my own children it was easier for me because I used to bathe that baby and she (the mother) just left that baby alone with me and the baby slept with me in my bed. She didn't get home until really late at night but that was really scary for me. It was really scary. But I don't know . . . she trusted me enough to do that. To me, that was a hard experience because I was a full-time maid, when I was originally just supposed to be a part-time domestic schoolgirl.

Eventually Chibby left the young couple and went to work at another house as a domestic worker. After high school, Chibby attended East Los Angeles

City College and would have to wake up at 5 A.M. in the morning to take the bus to get to her 8 A.M. class. Later, she registered for the Art Institute in Chicago and spent a semester taking classes there. Eventually, she came back to California and opened up a small food shop in Torrance, California. After a couple years she closed the shop and she decided to start a catering business with her daughter.

After Japanese Americans were released from the internment camps many of the young individuals similar to Chibby became domestic workers in White American households. Zia (2000) writes, "Still subjected to segregated housing and unequal treatment, young men and women who made it through high school and college could find work only as field hands and domestic workers, in the same limited occupations as their immigrant parents" (p. 39). The act of working in domestic, agricultural, and industrial fields post-World War II changed the identities of Japanese Americans.

Japanese American women like Yoshi, Toshi K., and Chibby, experienced a variety of jobs, ranging from working in a mess hall in the Poston internment camp to owning a catering company. All of these women worked from a young age throughout their adulthood, ventured through states and cities foreign to them, and great distances to accomplish entrepreneurship, education, and build their lives. Like most Americans of high school age, Japanese American teenagers did not usually have to work and live away from their parents at such a young age. Japanese Americans had to give up their houses and lost everything they owned prior to entering the internment camps, when they were released from the internment camps they did not have any homes, jobs, and financial security to return to, especially since many Americans possessed prejudiced feelings against Japanese Americans. Looking back on the labor and challenging circumstances of these three women, one can see the determination and strength they faced through some of the most difficult times of their lives.

Chapter 7

Pathways to Memories and Dancing Forward

Practicing a culture's arts such as poetry, dancing, painting, calligraphy, singing, flower arranging, and many other creative traditions can create pathways toward reconnecting with one's culture and memories. Art becomes a part of memory, tradition, culture, and identity. A painting can express a feeling, experience, a visual moment influenced by the contextual qualities of the artist and the time in which they lived. A song communicates tradition melodically and communicatively throughout time, embracing the meaning and values of the singer or musician. Researchers such as Phu (2008) and Tohe (1998) analyze photography and the writing of poetry to inquire deeper meanings about ethnic people's life experiences and the way arts interact with time, location, audience, and the artists.

Numerous Japanese Americans participated in various types of arts while in the internment camps. Hirasuna (2005, p. 24) wrote, "The making of arts and crafts in the relocation camps was both a physical and an emotional necessity for the internees." Whether individuals in the internment camp were making wooden birds, painting, or scrounging for materials to make furniture, there were all kinds of art that was created in the internment camps. The famous artist and sculptor Isamu Noguchi even spent some time in the Poston interment camp at Arizona, where he carved wooden masks while he was there. Dance, theatre, wood carving, and painting are some of the arts Japanese Americans participated in while interned in the various camps.

In Kramer's (2003) article "*Gaiatsu* and Cultural Judo," the Japanese culture and how Japan experienced outside pressure from the United States is examined. *Gaiatsu* is characterized from the Japanese point of view and its inevitable modernization influenced by Western countries (Kramer, 2003).

Kramer (2003) steps away from the assumption that one must de-culturize or un-learn himself or herself in order to experience the modern world. In order to gain a greater understanding of how Japanese viewed the inflow of Western influences, Kramer (2003) looks at the work from some of the country's most respected artists and researches Japanese culture using the work of some of Japan's greatest artists to reflect the transition of Japan's influence by the Western world in their process of modernization. Practicing traditional arts as a way of connecting or reconnecting with ones culture can teach a person so much about a culture's values, language, communication, and traditions, especially odori dance.

The youngest Japanese American woman I interviewed who was in the Japanese American internment camps was June Ito. She first began her lifelong journey as an odori dancer and now a respected teacher, in the internment camp. As I was working on this research about Japanese American women, I had also been taking private odori lessons from her, a certified odori *Sensei* (Japanese arts teacher) in Monterey Park, a neighborhood in Los Angeles. I arrived at the house of my Sensei on a sunny California winter morning. She greeted me at the door wearing both a warm smile and traditional tartan-design gold and red kimono made of wool. We walked into her studio, and slowly and gracefully (she, more so than I) bent down on our knees and bowed deeply, saying, "Oni-gai-wa-tashi-mas" to each other. We did a traditional odori dance, to the tune "Sakura (Cherry Blossoms)"and created an imaginary spring season day filled with falling cherry blossom petals through our movements. Throughout our dancing she would tell me brief stories of her life and travels to Japan. The more we danced, the more relaxed she became. The tamotos (long swinging sleeves of kimonos) slowly cut through the air like the cherry blossoms awakening in the springtime. When my Sensei, June, dances she is powerful though light and sensitive in her movements, and her skill and precision are expressed through her knowledge of Japanese female humbleness and graciousness. At the end of the dance we bowed to each other, deeply, and with both hands on the floor and said, "arigato gozimashta" which means "thank you very much."

June is the youngest of the Japanese American women who were in the World War II internment camps whom I have interviewed. She sees herself as part Nisei and part Sansei because on her father's side, she is second-generation, and on her mother's side she is third generation Japanese American. She possesses a talented and creative soul of a timeless traditional Japanese kabuki dancer, and more importantly, the knowledge of traditional Japanese arts.

She was born in 1940 in Los Angeles, California, and was only a young child when she was relocated into the internment camp. Although June was a very young age when she entered into the Manzanaar, California internment camp, the experience changed her life forever because it is where she first took odori lessons. June recalls:

> I had started Japanese dance when I was in the (Manzanaar) internment camp. I learned it from a lady, she wasn't certified but she had learned Japanese dance for a long time and she loved it, so she taught some of us it. That was my first exposure to it. I hardly remember that too though because I was only four years old. Basically, my mother was really anti-Japanese so she wasn't for it, but my father loved Japanese dance, and so did his mother so they're the ones who must've wanted that for me.

The events in June's family influenced her lifestyle and professional career as a traditional Japanese dance teacher. Her mother, a Nisei woman, was born in Burbank, California, and her father was born in Japan in 1906. His parents came to the U.S. after he was born, and summoned him to come live with them in the U.S. when he was 19 years old. He traveled from Japan by ship, but did not like the United States, so he went back to Japan. He came again to the United States a few years later, and for the second time, decided he did not want to stay in the United States. The third time he traveled to the United States, he was in his late-20s and decided to stay in America. He met June's mother when he was around 34 or 35 and she was 24 or 25, and they married even though there was a 10-year age difference between them.

Japanese familial surnames and status play a significant role in a person's lineage. June explains an issue in her Japanese American heritage:

> I don't know why she married an Issei person because she was so Americanized and she wanted to be so American. My father was supposedly very good looking, and she was also probably attracted to him cause he was a city-slicker. My father married into my mother's family. There were no males in her generation, and he married into her family name in order to carry the family last name or else her family would just disappear, like me, because I didn't marry and there's no one in my family and generation with my last name.

When World War II ended in 1945, June and her family returned to Los Angeles, both of her parents went to work and they moved into different apartments several times. June changed elementary schools nine times because it was so hard for her family to find an affordable apartment post-World War II. She remembers housing was a real problem and she had to live with her grandmother for a year in Los Angeles.

Throughout our discussion June mentioned her mother's anti-Japanese feelings often. I found this to be very surprising since June, my Japanese odori Sensei, knows and loves so many Japanese traditions. She did not

explain why her mother was anti-Japanese, but explained some of the overall
challenges of being from Japanese ancestry:

> I think because there was an anti-Japanese feeling because of the war. But
> even before the war, Japanese were not allowed to buy property. I think there
> was some kind of law about that and that's why Isseis couldn't buy property.
> The Niseis were eventually able to, the Isseis were not. I think the law was if
> you weren't a citizen then you couldn't buy property. I also think if you were a
> Nisei and you married someone from Japan, you also lost your citizenship. My
> Sensai said she had lost her citizenship even though she was born here and she
> had to be re-instated when she married her [Japanese] husband. But I think that
> was just prior to the war breaking out and there were already anti-Japanese feel-
> ings. The Japanese army was also in so many countries, like China; they were
> really viewed as the aggressor.

Though the Japanese traditional arts were not passed down to June from
mother to daughter, one Japanese woman played an important role in her life
and her decisions of practicing odori. After World War II June was growing
up as a teenager and she found it so difficult to live with her parents, specifically her mother, she decided to run away and pursue odori professionally.
She first learned odori in the Manzanaar internment camp, and as a teenager
and young adult, it changed her life. Although June's Japanese American
mother was very anti-Japanese in many ways and chose to not embrace her
own culture, June's father and his mother (June's grandmother) possessed an
appreciation for odori and introduced June to it as a young girl and it maintained a role in her life throughout time. June says:

> I got an AA degree. I wanted to get out of my house as much as possible because
> my mother and I were at each other's throats. I had gone to city college, got a
> job, I wanted to move out on my own but my father wouldn't let me because
> he said, all Japanese girls have to stay home until they're married. I had run
> away a couple of times; I was 19 years old. Then my Sensai intervened and
> said I should come stay with her to do Japanese dancing. The lady I originally
> learned Japanese dance from in the internment camp, she was not certified or
> anything like that and she only had so much ability, and the Sensai I moved in
> with was much more of a higher ranking, better, and obviously more talented.
> Japanese dance was an excuse for me to get out of the house, but my Sensai told
> me, at least it was a way for my father to save face, that I didn't just move out
> of the house and go to an apartment. He really didn't want me to move out and
> go to an apartment because I would be unsupervised.

June does not have many memories of the Japanese American internment
camp, but it is the place where she learned odori which has remained one of
the most important influences in her life even through all the anti-Japanese

feelings she felt in her environment while growing up. She was able to explain the difficulties and challenges her parents faced after World War II, finding jobs and a place to live while taking care of their children. The odori lessons her father and grandmother (her father's mother) introduced her to in the Manzanaar internment camp led her to a lifelong journey of practicing traditional Japanese arts, travels to Japan, and sharing her talents with others. She lived with her Sensai up until her Sensai's death, and still lives in her Sensai's house to this day. She is a professional and certified odori teacher and an artist of traditional Japanese arts. June has traveled to Japan and several places in the U.S. to teach her gift of odori.

Odori is viewed as a very intricate and complex art in Japanese culture. As an American-born and raised woman, June engaged in the Japanese culture through odori. Practicing traditional dancing gave her opportunities to travel and have immersive cultural arts experiences in Japan, and altered her identity as both a keeper and creator of Japanese traditional arts and Japanese American culture. In 2013 June brought her cultural arts knowledge to Los Angeles, where she choreographed the dancing in the Little Tokyo Nisei Week parade. She had choreographed and danced in the parade before and is well known throughout the Japanese American community. I had the pleasure of dancing with her in the Los Angeles Nisei Week parade and observed how she thoughtfully choreographed the dancing to represent the Japanese American community. Using both American and Japanese flags, we did beautiful dances representing our multicultural identities. Zia (2000) writes, "The responsibility of identifying which cultural traditions to maintain ultimately falls on the generation that grows up straddling the traditional and American cultures" (p. 262). Through performing arts such as dance, singing, music, and acting, the culture gains visibility via some of its most authentic and traditional practices in American locations and spaces.

Chapter 8

After the Internment Camps

Internal Strength, Support, and Friendships

The United States government gradually released the Japanese American prisoners from the internment camps. Families were split apart and individuals were selected for various jobs. Most all of the Japanese American women who were in the internment camps and interviewed for this project were separated from their families after they exited the internment camps and eventually were able to reunite with their families a few years later. Some of the internees' brothers and cousins joined the U.S. military to fight for the United States as a way of showing their loyalty to their country. In coherence to the study conducted by Nagata and Cheng (2003), they wrote about how suicides took place especially among the elderly Japanese Americans who felt the shame and stress of having to start over again. For many Japanese American people, the internment camp experience was very traumatic, even when they were released from the internment camps. Toshi T. remembered:

> When we were let out from camp, some of us were given $100 to start our lives over again. Some people weren't even given that, it was very difficult to find work. My cousin, who had graduated from the University of California, Berkeley, couldn't find a job and was so depressed. He eventually hung himself.

Most of the women in this study went to school and work immediately after they were released from the internment camps. The majority of the women in this research were only teenagers when they left camp and traveled across the United States by themselves to find jobs. As I was writing this book in 2007, my grandmother received her high school diploma from the Bureau of Indian Affairs, since the Poston internment camp was located on the Colorado River Indian Reservation in Arizona. She was in her early 80s when the diploma arrived in the mail, she smiled and said, "Oh hey! Look at that!" She held up the diploma to show it to me. Her eyes got a little watery and then she smiled.

"I'm not sure why they're sending this to me now," she said, "but it looks like I finally received my diploma!"

For the Issei, Nisei, and some of the Sansei generations of women who grew up in the 1940s, it was uncommon for Japanese American women to leave their families' home until they got married. The World War II internment camps broke this tradition because it became a necessity for young Japanese American women to work to help their families and support themselves. My grandfather's younger sister, Sachiko said:

> When Jerome closed, we went to another camp that was in Arkansas and we went to Rohwer and we stayed there for over a year. In 1945, we came back to Boyle Heights and that's when my mother's half-sister, found us a house. I was 14, and I was going to junior high school. I went to Roosevelt High School. Most people were like us. We lost our farm and everything and we couldn't go back because nothing was the same.

Throughout the years after World War II, Japanese American women faced a lot of racism and numerous challenges after they exited the internment camps. Even though many Japanese Americans felt a sense of shame about their internment camp experiences, several Japanese Americans, such as Sachiko, are also very patriotic. In her interviews she talked a lot about writing to different men in the military who she was pen pals with and had lifelong friendships. She has always seen herself as an American and supports the U.S Marines, Army, and Navy servicewomen and men and all the work they do for the U.S.

MULTIDIMENSIONS OF GENERATIONAL, ETHNIC, AND GENDER COMMUNICATION

My extended family and I are sitting at the dinner table in my grandmother's (my father's mother) dining room. The place settings are all properly laid out and inclusive of all of the utensils one could use to eat a meal; it looks orderly and uniform with a warm and homey touch. The dishes, cups, napkins, spoons, knives, and forks create a framing border around the delicious homemade food lying in the center of the table. We are having another pleasant family dinner and I am happy to see many of my family members and my relatives. My grandmother is sitting to the right of me and my brother is sitting on my left-hand side. She turns to me and says, "Please serve your brother his food." The chicken and vegetables are equal distance from both my brother and I. I don't mind serving people at all, whether they are female or male, especially when the food is closer to me and difficult for the other person to reach, but at this moment the chicken is right in front of both my brother and I.

My brother, who at that time was a young and very able man at 25 years old, says to our grandmother, "Oh no, it's ok I can serve myself." He and I have a very good relationship and enjoy spending time together. My brother is one of the closest people in my life. We did not grow up in a household with my parents where I was taught to serve him because he is male or because I am a few years older.

My grandmother turns to my brother without looking at me and says, "No, no." She looks at me and says, "Let her serve you, she wants to serve you." I do not make any kind of face nor roll my eyes, nor say any snappy reply back to my grandmother because I know it would be disrespectful and I love her very much. I know she loves me too, and I never doubt how much she cares for both my brother and I. I take my brother's plate and put two pieces of chicken on it, some vegetables, mashed potatoes, and a bread roll. At that moment it does not seem like the appropriate time for one of my scholarly monologues about gender equality at the dinner table. I respect my grandmother and have always learned it is not polite to talk back to your grandparents, even though my years of women's studies classes and courses on gender, ethnicity, sexuality, and power and privilege are bubbling inside me. However, this is truly an example of gender, ethnicity, and generation. My Japanese value of respecting your elders at this moment supersedes over my confusion about her perspectives on gender and a flood of silent negotiations and emotions takes place inside of me after the dinner as I reflect upon it.

A few minutes later, my confusion dissolves and fades away. I realized there is so much I do not know about my grandmother's life and I have never lived through the times she did, nor have I had all the experiences she has had. There are reasons she does this, it is not because she loves my brother more or likes males more or says things like this because she is a Japanese American woman, but a lot of it has to do with generation and her own social norms. Culturally and generationally, she interacts differently with males than I do. I know many Japanese American women in my family do not serve their husbands or the males in our family, especially the women of my parents' generation and later, like myself.

If some people were to read the description of the incident between my grandmother on my father's side of my family, my brother, and I during our family dinner where she requests for me to "please serve your brother," she or he may think my grandmother is just being old-fashioned, sexist, even a bit cruel, or perhaps just being "Japanese" in coherence to whatever stereotypes they have about Japanese women. The reason why it is important for me to look at and analyze this incident is because my grandmother is anything but old-fashioned, sexist, or cruel. On the contrary, she is very modern, has a deep appreciation for the women around her, and is extremely nice, gracious, and polite. Out of all my relatives, she is also one of the most well-traveled, independent, cultured, and active.

The incidents that cause family members to view each other's actions and words at superficial levels can contribute to arguments, burned bridges, and misunderstandings. It has been important for me to learn about my grandmother's past in order to make sense of some of her values, accomplishments, beliefs, and identities that she possesses in the present. I decide to interview her for this project so I can learn more about my grandmother as a woman, who I know wants the best for my brother and I and shows it in ways we sometimes cannot always understand. My interview with my grandmother on my father's side shows how her values, generation, and identity relates to Japanese American women's life experiences, responsibilities, and generation.

Halualani (2002) writes, "discussions speak to the complex arena of identity as more than self-recognitions, natural essences, or invented traditions," and to observe "how we are, as social-historical subjects, related to power in terms of the structural forces that invisibly inscribe how we see and enact 'who are we'?" (p. xxiii). As family members, my grandmother and I have so many characteristics in common such as we love to travel, socialize, dance, and are active. However, if I ask, "who are we?" I know we have our differences as Japanese American women because of our histories, experiences, and the contexts in which we have grown up throughout time.

My grandmother, Michi, grew up in Los Angeles during the late 1920s. Her father worked in the furniture department at Robinson's department store and her mother did intricate hand-sewing at home and cared for her family. When she was in the 10th grade in high school she and her family were evacuated to the Santa Anita racetrack assembly center. She and other Japanese American teenagers her age contributed to the U.S. war effort by helping make and repair camouflage nets. After living in the horse stables of Santa Anita, my grandmother and her family were relocated to the internment camps in Rohwer, Arkansas, where she attended school, made friends, danced, and painted a famous mural in the internment camp's auditorium. My grandmother's father left the internment camp to work in Minnesota and later, he sent for her to come out to Minnesota. She tells me about her journey to Minnesota:

> I got to Minneapolis, and you know, I don't know how much money I had, I think it was only $50 or something and I didn't know any better and I got a cab from the train station and I had him take me to the hostel, which was a place for people to stay. When I got there it was about 12:30 am or 1:00 am and the cab driver dropped me off and I went up to this door, and I walked in. I remember I was really thirsty so I drank a cup of water at the sink, and I didn't want to disturb anyone so I fell asleep on the couch. And this fella came home from work

Figure 8.1   Four Generations of Japanese American Women at a Party in the 1970s

and he worked at the Minneapolis Tribune and he walked in the door and saw
me sleeping. I guess he was so shocked, he said, "What are you doing here?"
But isn't it stupid to be in a strange house, in strange city and just fall asleep?
(laughs). He said that was the first time someone had forgot to lock the door, so
I was lucky. And he was a copy editor or something for the Tribune. We were all
people from camp that didn't have any place to stay at that time. My girlfriend
Jennie came from Poston, and she joined me there.

A few weeks after I had interviewed my grandmother about her World
War II internment camp experience, she called me and said her best friend,
Jennie, would be interested in being interviewed for my research project. I
had already met Jennie several times; she is like family to us. We know her
as being my grandmother's closest friend and she is also very artistic and
creative. She and my grandmother's lives overlap and they have shared so
many significant moments together, which helps me to understand why their
friendship is so deep.

I met Jennie at her house in Gardena. Her story was filled with moments
she shared with my grandmother after camp:

I left camp in June of '44 to Minneapolis to join my good friend Michi
(laughs). . . . Because Michi was going there [to Minneapolis] and her mother
was going there, my mother finally gave in because she realized we'd have adult

supervision. I was in Minneapolis for maybe 15 or 16 months. I got a job at the Bemus bag factory, making sacks for potatoes. I went to work there, I went to the employment office and got a job there. But the material that they use is so coarse that when you're sewing it rips your blouse because it would shred it. So anyways, I think I worked there only a couple of weeks cause I was looking for a secretarial job so I got a job at a small metal manufacturer company and I worked there in a small office. And of course the people I worked for never had a Japanese or Asian employee and they didn't even know anything about evacuation. They were mostly Norwegian and Swedish.

Throughout the interviews with my grandmother, Michi, and her best friend, Jennie, I began to understand why they were such close best friends and realized how much they went through together. They both had to grow up very quickly as teenagers after World War II and had a lot of responsibilities at such a young age. They did not have the carefree lives that most teenagers experience, instead they were working in factories, struggling to find housing, and helping their parents with expenses. The experiences they had after the World War II internment camps revealed how they relied on each other for more than just companionship but through survival and hardships. For my grandmother, her best friend, Jennie, played an important and supportive role throughout her challenges after the internment camps:

When Jennie and I decided that it was time to move [out of the hostel] I got a job at Nabisco because my friend was working there and I packed crackers (laughs) on the assembly line. Gosh, I think we were paid $0.75 an hour, something ridiculous and Jennie got a job in an office doing clerical work. So we decided to move out, and at that time there was a shortage of housing and we found one room in a house and I remember the mattress was made of straw and we had one hot plate and we used to go out to eat but it was too expensive so Jennie decided we were going to have some dinners at home. We bought rice, they didn't have rice cookers in those days so we cooked it in the pot and I remember her mother sent umeboshi and funyou. Do you know what funyou is? That fermented tofu? And she would eat that, and I would say, "ohmigod, how can you eat that? It's so smelly!" But by god, I learned to like it! (laughs). That would be our dinner sometimes—umeboshi, rice, and funyou (pickled vegetable)! But that was our life.

When my grandmother's mother finally left the internment camp, she came to Minneapolis. My grandmother, her mother, and her sister-in-law moved into a rented "backside of a house" where there were two bedrooms, a kitchen, and a bathroom. Her brother was in the U.S. military at that time, stationed in Minnesota. My grandmother remembered how her mother would feed other Japanese Americans coming out of the internment camps and had them stay with her and her family in their small rented residence. I began to understand the importance and value of hospitality to my grandmother as she told me this.

When my grandmother was still a teenager, she faced one of the most difficult and responsible challenges of her life when she found out her mother had cancer. My grandmother and her family were still living in very minimal and sparse conditions at the time. Financial stability was a struggle in their household. She says:

> A couple of years later, my mother found out she had cancer. She had stomach pains. When Jennie first came out of camp, because she didn't have a job, she took my mother to a doctor and they found out she had cancer and she began receiving treatment. I remember giving her a bath at night and she weighed only about 70 lbs., just skin and bones. I would carry her to the bathtub and I was only 17 or 18 years old (voice saddens). The doctor predicted that she would die within that year. So when my brother left to Monterey, he told me, "mom may not last," but she fooled all the doctors, lived to be almost 95, the doctor passed away before she did. She was an amazing woman.

After interviewing my grandmother, Michi, and her best friend, Jennie, I was thankful Jennie volunteered to be a participant in this research. So much of the support my grandmother received during post-World War II came from Jennie. Likewise, much of Jennie's narrative consisted of moments and experiences with my grandmother. The bond between these two Japanese American women displayed how much Japanese American family, friends, and women relied on and helped each other post-World War II. Had this been a survey, I would have not seen the specific ways in which each woman spoke of one another with so much sincerity and love. The moments when a person's voice saddens or when they laugh, play important roles in their narratives, because one can also see how they are reacting to their memories and experiences they have had.

My grandmother's experiences as a teenager taking care of her mother with cancer, carrying her into the bathtub, and supporting her through her treatment revealed the amount of responsibility and emotional strength she had to possess at such a young age. By the time she was the age I am now as I write this, I realize she had already been married and had two children. To her, a young woman takes care of those around her and is a caretaker to the elderly, her husband, and her children. When she was in her twenties my grandfather was working out of state and she was already taking care of her two children on her own.

After Japanese Americans were released from the internment camps some of the Japanese American women enrolled into the public high schools while they worked jobs on the side so they could earn their high school diplomas after they left the internment camps. Many of the Japanese American women in this book worked as domestic workers, and some eventually worked in factories after the war. Post-World War II, American society was still very racist against Japanese Americans, regardless of their citizenship, skills, or educational level. Numerous Japanese Americans had to work full-time jobs just to receive the minimum amount of financial support to survive and few of the women interviewed in this project were able to attend college.

The challenges Japanese Americans faced after the war lasted for several years. They struggled not only financially and emotionally, but also to regain acceptance as U.S. American citizens. Several years after World War II ended, Michi spoke about how she and her husband came to Los Angeles to buy a house. When the neighbors heard that Japanese American people were going to move into the vacant house, they had a neighborhood meeting to discuss the "dangers" of Japanese Americans moving into the area. She states:

> They said we shouldn't buy in this area because Japanese were not . . . they were discouraged, because it was an all-White area. But this lady that had this house was having a feud with her neighbors so she just sold it to the first person who came along. So at one time, I found out the neighbors were so upset, I had been talking to Marci's [her daughter] friends' parents, I became close with one, especially, and she told me that they had a block meeting after we moved in because they were so afraid that because of us prices would go down, and yeah . . . there was so much prejudice. But we were unaware of all that. We were from Minneapolis so we just bought it. There were no Japanese in this area at the time.

When my grandmother, Michi, and her family moved into the neighborhood, she and her family did not even know racism existed against them until several years later. Throughout time her neighbors accepted her and her family. Some of the neighbors thought having Japanese American people moving into an all-White neighborhood threatened the value of the property due to their racial presence.

Interviewing my grandmother helped me to understand how our life experiences have been so different. Halualani (2002) writes about how Hawaiians have gone through social and historical changes and these transformations are what contribute to their identities. This concept is similar with Japanese American women. World War II and the internment camps had historical, social, educational, national, and financial effects on the Japanese American women like my grandmother. The conditions of the interwar era transformed Japanese American teenagers into the roles of responsible adults, caretakers, and laborers. In my early thirties, I have had the opportunity to have a variety of jobs, live in different countries, and go to graduate school, but for her, she developed a greater and more gracious strength of caring for the people around her and being a mother. Sure, sometimes my grandmother interacts with males differently than females, as many people may do without even noticing, due to a combination of generation, culture, and life experiences. When my grandmother asks me to serve my brother I believe she is not telling me to do so not only because he is a male, it is because she hopes I can develop the selflessness and values of hospitality she acquired during her young adulthood years.

Chapter 9

Japanese Americans and Japanese Peruvians as Hostages

Many Japanese American women have not told their experiences and life stories to their children and grandchildren. From my own experience, my grandparents (my mother's parents) told my brother and I in great detail about their lives in the internment camp as we grew older. They did not tell us when we were small children but eventually as teenagers and young adults my brother and I found them speaking about it more and more. We had noticed they had not told our parents much about their internment camp experiences and I was always surprised my father had no desire to visit Japan, though my mother spoke often about her trip to Japan when she was a teenager. When I spoke to several of the Japanese American women in this research, I found some of their answers to be similar to their answers of when I asked about their communication with their children. One of the women, Grace, says:

> I don't think I've told them [our grandchildren]. If anything, I think my kids would tell them. But they never asked me about it. It was never like, I'm going to sit down and tell you about life and camp. So actually, I don't know if they're interested. I've heard there's very little of it in the history books. So I don't really know . . . I don't know how much they know or how curious they are, because maybe they think we don't want to talk about it. Could that be? It was a black era in our lives. But actually in my life it wasn't black, because if it wasn't for that . . . well, when you don't have anything, everything is good, right? Everything is good. I mean we never had any of this stuff, our own furniture, and we just made due with what we had.

Most Japanese American women in this book explained their experiences with elements of sadness but most spoke with a sense of strength, pride, and American patriotism. The "interlocking axes of power" are not divided between their Japanese identities and their American identities but are situated in contextual, historicized, and socialized ongoing negotiations between embracing their Japanese traditions and American patriotism (Shome, 1999, p. 109). When I spoke to my grandmother on my father's side and asked if she had told her story to any of her children or grandchildren, she said to me, "No, you're the only one who asked about our family history."

Many people in my family remember how my grandfather (my father's father) talked about some of his experiences during World War II in the form of entertaining stories, especially one particular story about how he drove his brand new car onto the Poston, Arizona internment camp site where his parents and his brother were imprisoned. It was an internment camp where supposedly "dangerous" Japanese Americans were held. My great-grandparents who were in that internment camp were far from dangerous. My grandfather had driven his brand new car into the internment camp and the guards confiscated his car. He was unable to get his car back, and he would tell this story often throughout his life.

The story of my grandfather (my father's father) relates to Azuma's (2009) research on Japanese American Nisei (second-generation) men who were chick-sexers throughout the 1930s and 1950s. From my mother's side of the family, I am a fifth-generation Japanese American, but from my father's side of the family, I am a fourth-generation Japanese American. From January until around June, my grandfather on my father's side, would go to Minnesota and work as a chick-sexer, separating the cockerels (male chicks) from the pullets (female chicks) for egg farmers. Azuma's (2009) research focuses on this area of employment that is also part of my family's history.

Japanese Americans played a significant role in the chick-sexing industry because they were racially "considered suited for this important task, but scientific studies during the time in the 1940s also explained that their other 'racial' traits, like dexterity, small fingers, and physical endurance, would allow Nisei practitioners to avoid ruining baby chickens" as they were being examined (Azuma, 2009, p. 244). I'm doubtful my grandfather had dexterity or small fingers, but chick-sexing was a job accessible and open to Japanese Americans because of such ethnic-related beliefs previously mentioned. My grandfather was living in Minnesota when the Executive Order 9066 took place and all the Japanese Americans had to be removed from the west coast. He did not have to enter into the internment camps immediately because he was already living in Mankato, Minnesota. After the chick-sexing season was over in summer, he drove to the Poston, Arizona, internment camp in his brand new car where his family was and then he was imprisoned there too. The guards never returned his brand new car back to him.

Throughout the interviews, stories about various people and generations in the Japanese American women's lives would arise in our conversations.

When one of the women, Kinue, and I were discussing the communication between her and her grandchildren, she mentioned:

> My biggest regret is not asking my mother what life was like coming to this country. They have the series on TV about the war. I haven't had time to look at TV, but this is what we experienced. We didn't know what was going on but it was nice to know about it after. My mother was in Hiroshima and her father was a womanizer and an alcoholic and she was the only child. No money. So she was left with her grandmother and her parents went to Hawaii to work in this plantation. So after she went to middle school, her grandmother said, "You're going to America as a picture-bride." Oh boy. She was only 16 years old. She went on the boat and came to America. She said to me so many of the guys would find younger guys, good-looking guys, and send their pictures. When the women would come to America they would say, "Ohmigod, where's the man?" She said some of the gals who had money, would turn around and go back home. She didn't have a choice. So she stayed in America. It turns out this guy, I don't know how old he was—he was an alcoholic. She had one little boy, then her husband died from alcoholism. She had one boy whom I think he got killed on a tricycle bike that was hit by a car.
>
> So here's my mother in America, with no education, she could barely speak the language, and I think she worked the grape fields in the Fresno area. Then the marriage broker put my mom and dad together. Now, when they did that my father's family disowned him because they were quite wealthy and didn't approve of what he was doing.

The lives of many of the women I interviewed consisted of sad stories and struggles that they and their parents faced. Their route toward empowerment does not come from a postcolonial framework, viewing themselves as victims or powerless because of their colonized histories. Instead, they are able to use their knowledge and strength they have gained to move forward and change their lives, even if it meant not looking back.

Not all Japanese American women kept their stories silent. There is one woman in particular who has shared her story with her children, grandchildren, and the public; her name is Reiko. As I was driving to Reiko's house in South Central Los Angeles, I did not know what to expect from her story. She was one of the first people I interviewed for this project since I was referred to her by one of my family members. We had never met until the day of the interview though I have known her daughter since I was a baby. I entered her house and she had a plate of cookies waiting there for me. She welcomed me graciously into her home and we sat at her table.

Reiko was born in Los Angeles in 1928. Her father owned a wholesale produce market in downtown Los Angeles. When she was nine years old in 1937, she went on her first trip to Japan with her family. At first, I was not sure why she was telling me so many details about her trip to Japan, but the details of her Japan trip are important to the events that occurred later in her narrative. She said:

> My dad took us as a whole family [to Japan] because he wanted us to get our tonsils out and he didn't have much faith in the American doctors. We combined it with a sightseeing trip, so we there for about six weeks but we spent two weeks in the hospital just to get our tonsils taken out because we were foreigners and they were treating us really good, like celebrities. So after our tonsils were out we traveled through Kyushu and he wanted to show us the different places in Kyushu and this was from summer into a part of a school semester in fall.

In Reiko's narrative the purpose of her family's trip to Japan reveals its significance. Because of her family's medical and sightseeing trip to Japan in 1937, the United States government later suspected Reiko's father of suspicious activity during World War II. Thus, a long sad and surprising story of how their family was separated and then taken to Japan as U.S. hostages is told from her perspective and experiences. From the beginning of her story, I was expecting her to tell a narrative very similar to the other few women I had interviewed, but her story started to sound very different. She said:

> In 1941, after the war broke out, December 7, at 7:30 P.M., two FBI agents and a policeman came and arrested my father that evening, so we didn't know where he was for a couple of weeks. It was scary because my mother was only in her early 30s with four kids and the eldest was only fifteen and a half. I really marvel that she was able to handle what she did. There was an English teacher at Poly High [School] that my cousin was going to and she had heard about all these fathers being taken after Pearl Harbor, so she made it a point to find out where they were. My brother had a learner's driving permit so he drove my mother and my auntie, and they [the fathers] were being held at Terminal Island. They could see my father, but the guards wouldn't let them speak to him. Eventually, my mother was told to pack clothing for him for both cold weather and hot weather. We found out after Terminal Island, he came over right here to the jail in Los Angeles, on the top floor of the hall of records off the freeway. I understand they were held there for a short while, and then from there they were sent to Missoula, Montana. During that time, we were still here in Los Angeles because we hadn't been interned yet.

Terminal Island is located in San Pedro, California, slightly south of Los Angeles. It is a man-made island in an industrial port area owned by the Port of Los Angeles. Terminal Island became a temporary prison location, confining Japanese American men during the evacuation.

In the spring of 1942, Reiko and her family were relocated to the Santa Anita assembly center at the Santa Anita horse racetrack like many other

Japanese Americans. While her mother, brothers, and she were at the assembly center, Reiko's father was placed in a men's-only justice camp. Reiko's father had to stay in the justice camp while she and the rest of her family were relocated to the Amache internment camp in Colorado. Reiko felt it was important to describe her father and his character in order for me to gain more insight about their situation:

> My dad is the type of person who is very family-oriented. On September 1, 1943, we left camp. My father thought that he was going to die in camp if he couldn't be with his family, and he was told he could go to Japan and then that way the family could be together. Actually, he really wanted to go to Crystal City which was a family [internment] camp but it was full and they couldn't accommodate him, so he signed up to go to Japan to be with the family.

Their family was denied the opportunity to go to the Crystal City, Texas, family internment camp. Reiko's father had never committed any crime or participated in any illegal activity throughout his entire lifetime, but the family's medical trip in Japan made them suspects to the United States of being potentially dangerous. Reiko and her family signed up for the government's program to go to Japan. They were not given many details or explanations of what kind of program it was. She says:

> Later on we found out the reason for that was we were being exchanged for other Americans. So the more Japanese Americans they could get on the ship, the more they could exchange us for the Americans that were trapped over there [in Japan] so they could come home. You know, my father and mother were legal immigrants, my three brothers and I were American citizens, so in other words they were exchanging American citizens of Japanese ancestry for American citizens of White ancestry. A lot people have not heard of this story. We went on the Swedish liner, which was a neutral country and the ship was called Gripsholm. We went across the Atlantic Ocean, stopped at two ports in South America in Rio de Janeiro and Montevideo and then we swung around Africa at Port Elizabeth and then we went up to Goa, India, and that's where the Japanese liner with the Americans were on, and they literally exchanged human cargo—humans and baggage—we were there for one day. On the Japanese liner we stopped in Singapore and Manila, and we were able to go ashore there because it was occupied by the Japanese army. Then we went to Kobe and from there, Yokohama. I was 15 years old at that time. I had kept a diary but at that time my brother said they were confiscating everything so I had to toss it overboard into the ocean and here I had this journal that I kept everyday about what we did, what happened, and now when I think about it, I think what a waste, you know? It took us from September 1, 1943 to November 17, 1943 to get to Yokohama. We went three quarters away around the world because we couldn't cross the Pacific Ocean.

While the family was en route to Japan, as Reiko had mentioned, the Swedish liner stopped in India where the exchange took place. Reiko tells me a short story about how the exchange was literally, "head for head." She recalls, there was one man who was on their ship as a hostage and he was in the mental ward of the ship because he had mental and physical disabilities. At one point before the exchange took place, the man got away from his supervising nurse and he wheeled his wheelchair over the railing. The ship's crew threw out life jackets into the sea and lowered a life boat down and people were looking for him. His body was nowhere to be found during that time and that affected the outcome of the exchange because there was one person missing.

Throughout the interview, I noticed Reiko was able to tell her story very matter-of-factly and was able to remember very specific details, such as exact dates. She explains:

> The sad story is the United States kidnapped some Japanese people living in Peru and they brought them over to the United States, put them in camp and they used them also to exchange. See, they are the ones that are fighting for redress. I did get redress after two years (after it was issued), I had to fight for mine because I had gone to an enemy's country during the war. What are you going to do if you're a minor? You have to go with your parents. Unless they wanted to make arrangements to stay, I would have gladly stayed. It took me two years with the help of the NCRR, they took me to Washington D.C., I spoke my case, and after two years they finally gave me my $20,000.

Reiko's participation with the National Coalition for Redress and Reparations (NCRR) encouraged her to remember and write down all the specific details of her experiences before, during, and after World War II. She has spoken about the hostage program she and her family joined several times when she had to fight to obtain her redress sum from the government. After Reiko and her family were exchanged as hostages in India, they were taken to Japan. She says:

> I was in Japan until 1947. I was there four years. I was there for two years during the war, and then two years after and I worked for the Air Force base. They had schooling but after about six months the school was bombed. We didn't have a school anymore. I think all this has helped me to cope with a lot of things. It took me three or four months to finally understand what the teacher was saying [in Japanese] because my Japanese was just conversational with my parents. Until you go to Japan, you don't realize there are a lot of words you don't know. When you talk to the Isseis (first generation Japanese Americans) here you're throwing in a lot of American words which they understand but in Japan, everything has to be pure Japanese. It was very difficult. It was an experience.

In Japan, it was very difficult for Reiko to go to the Japanese state-run school. Although Reiko was Japanese American, the Japanese language and transition of suddenly attending a school in a different country was very challenging. Reiko's mother eventually enrolled her into a school run by missionaries. The principal of the missionary school was a graduate from Boston College in the United States and spoke English. The missionary school was an all-girls high school and she attended it for about six months before she started working.

Aside from Reiko's challenges of going to school, during the time of World War II Japan was having food and resource shortages. She says:

> By the time we got to Japan, Japan didn't have a lot of young people because they were all involved with the war. They didn't have much food. We were rationed with brown rice and with the brown rice, they would give us dried daikon, rolled barley, and dried sweet potato and my mother would cook that in with the brown rice. And then we had one loaf of bread for a family of five—for a week—of course no butter, no milk, no eggs, and so it got to the point that when my mother would go to the market, she would never buy [red] meat, she would only buy fish because she didn't know what the source of the meat was. She grew sweet potatoes and she would cook them and even the leaves she would cook into futomaki. She made use of every part of the sweet potato.

As I listened to Reiko tell her story, we sat at her dining room table eating cookies and drinking tea. Her husband walked around the house and every once in a while smiled at us. I realized even though she and her husband had both probably been through so much during and after World War II, they lived very relaxed, happy, and comfortable lives. Reiko went on to explain how she was able to make it back to the United States:

> Then when I came back to the United States in 1947, I had just turned 19 and I brought my 15-year-old brother with me by myself because my parents couldn't come. In order to get a passport I had to have someone vouch for me. There were a lot of G.I.'s that we knew that had gone to Japan on the occupation force so one of them came down to Fukoa to visit us. I went back to Yokohama with one of them and he took me to the Consulate in Yokohama and he vouched for me. He said that he knew me for over 10 years, we lived on the same street, and with that they gave me a special passport to return to the United States with my brother.

> When we got back to the United States, the first thing I wanted to do was enroll in high school. I didn't have a high school education. We had to have a financial sponsor so one of our good family friends took us in for two months and after that my brother and I did school boy and school girl work, which is you live at someone's home and for $30 they give you room and board and you do work around the house and they give you enough time so you can go to school.

I enrolled my brother in high school and I wanted to go to high school too but they said I was too old. They suggested I go to city college, so I went over to Los Angeles City College and took the entrance exam and got accepted. Some how, the records got mixed up and I never got my GED, but I did graduate and I received an AA degree.

In 1955 Reiko's parents and the rest of her family were finally able to make it back to the United States It took a long time for Reiko and her brother to get her parents and family back into the country. They had to hire a lawyer, and what Reiko finds most interesting about her parents coming back to the United States is:

You know, you think my father would be bitter but as soon as they were allowed to become citizens, my father went down and became a citizen. Isn't that something? I don't know if I could do that, a country that did something like that to me. Before that, they were not allowed to become citizens and they were not allowed to hold real estate.

Reiko's mother and father both chose to become U.S. citizens even with the hardships they went through and the politicized history that immobilized them from their freedom, family, and country for ten years. Their patriotism was displayed in the most complex of ways embedded in Japanese American history contextualized by politics, citizenship, and devotion to their country. This act should not be mistaken as shame of being Japanese or as passiveness but as a claim of rejecting an ongoing life of victimization as colonized individuals. They saw themselves as neither the colonizer nor the colonized; rather, they see their experiences as hostages as their ultimate contribution to America and the war effort. They did not know at the time what was truly happening during World War II, since the United States did not provide them with the knowledge and power necessary to fully understand what they were agreeing to.

In this project, I use this as an example of the "historical colonial separation" Gandhi (2006, p. 4) mentions. Reiko and her parents lived their lives with embedded qualities of colonization steeped into their identities, but from their point of view, they also contributed the greatest act of patriotism through the hostage exchange program.

Unlike many of the Japanese American women I spoke to Reiko tells me she talks about her experience often to her children and grandchildren:

I talk to my grandsons about this. The reason I talk about my experiences is because there are a lot of people in my generation, and they don't want to speak about their experiences, but the reason I do is I was sort of the spokesperson for the hostages. When I was appearing in these community programs and speaking about my experiences and why I felt I should get redress, Lucy and Lisa [her daughters] were very interested and whenever they would see any clippings they would clip it out because they wanted their boys to find out and know about my experiences. They know my husband's experiences; he was in the occupation force in Japan, but not for too long. He wanted to keep a scrapbook so when the boys grew up they knew what our history was. The Gripsholm took two trips. One was shortly after 1942 and that ship was filled with people from the embassy and people who were with big Japanese companies and then when the second one was being formed they didn't have too many left and that's why they got the Latin Americans, the Japanese from Peru. Some of them did get redress, but many of them, they didn't have the proper papers and I could understand that. I didn't have papers but I was fortunate the Consulate gave me my passport. There are really a lot of people that don't know about this exchange program. It's part of the U.S. history that is very shameful, you know, putting us into camps, taking our fathers away, shipping us Americans to Japan so other Americans could come back.

World War II created a tremendous lifelong impact on Reiko and her family's lives. The challenges she faced began when World War II started, from when her father was imprisoned and her family was evacuated into the internment camps, to when her family was taken hostage by the United States for the hostage exchange program. The colonization did not end there, Reiko had to struggle through difficult times in Japan with her family, find a way to come back to the United States with her brother, and start their lives over again without their parents in the United States with her brother. In 1955, ten years after World War II ended, her parents were finally allowed back into the United States Several decades later, Reiko had to fight for her redress since the government said she had not been in the U.S. Japanese American internment camps.

Daniels, Taylor, and Kitano (1986) write, "It is difficult to date with any kind of precision the start movement for redress" (p. 188). The battle for redress started in the late 1940s or some say in the late 1960s, when small groups and organizations of Japanese Americans began dialogues on reparations for their experiences during World War II (Daniels, Taylor, & Kitano, 1986). The redress movement was complicated and brought several Japanese Americans and organizations together. In 1978, the Japanese American Citizen League (JACL) initiated the beginnings of the movement (Tateishi, 1986) and in May 1979, the National Council for Japanese American Redress (NCJAR) was formed in Seattle (Hohri, 1986). On June 16, 1983, under the Ronald Reagan administration and Congress, the Commission on Wartime Relocation and Internment of Civilians issued recommendations for "each surviving victim of the exclusion and internment be compensated $20,000 as a redress for the injustice" (Tateishi, 1986, p. 195). Iwamura (2007) argues, "Although the Civil Liberties Act brought a great deal of closure," it did not completely mend the amount of prejudice Japanese Americans faced, as the memories of "internment remains ever present for many Nikkei" (p. 943).

I remember when I was a young girl and my grandparents received their checks for the redress. Some Japanese Americans decided to do as my grandparents did, travel or pass the money on to their grandchildren so their future generations could go to college. Whether it was the decision to travel and see the world or send their grandchildren to college, many Japanese Americans were now participating in opportunities that they never had when they were teenagers or young adults in the internment camps and after they were released from the internment camps. All four of my grandparents never had the opportunity to go to college because the moment they were released from the internment camps, they had no home to return to and had to work in factories, as domestics, and live in hostels or boarding houses for several years.

Through Reiko's story I was able to link her narrative to published research and literature regarding the Japanese Peruvians and Japanese Americans interned and exchanged as hostages by the United States Gardiner's (2001) research on the Japanese—U.S. hostage exchange also emphasizes how numerous Latin American Japanese people were forced into this exchange. Gardiner (2001) writes "the U.S. desire to retrieve the many American civilians in Japanese hands, the desire of Latin American governments to rid themselves of un-wanted aliens" (p. 144). United States Americans, Costa Ricans, and Peruvians of Japanese descent were aboard the Gripsholm liner that Reiko mentioned in her narrative (Gardiner, 1991). In the novel *Adios to Tears: The Memoirs of a Japanese-Peruvian in U.S. concentration camps* (Higashide, Gardiner, Kudo, 2002), Seiichi Higashide writes about his experiences, along with 2,200 other Japanese Latin Americans, who were shipped, taken from their homes, and interned by the U.S. government.

Individuals such as Reiko and some Japanese Americans from the United States and Japanese Latin Americans who participated in the hostage exchange program were originally excluded from the redress due to unclear documentation of them being in the internment camps. She and other Japanese Americans had to share their narratives in court and were eventually given their redress checks, though several Japanese Latin Americans who were also forced to participate in the exchange only received $5,000 in the *Mochizuki et al. v. United States* case in 1996 (Inada, 2000). The stories Reiko shared with her children and grandchildren bring to light a new sense of knowledge about U.S. history that for most people, has been unheard of and silenced. She uses this knowledge toward empowering her family, Japanese Americans, and all people about the lives of Japanese North Americans and Japanese Latin Americans during and after World War II.

Chapter 10

Rebuilding the American Dream

It was the fall season of 2007 and I was sitting at home one evening watching the DVD *American Pastime*. This film is about Japanese Americans in the Topaz relocation camp in Utah. There was an eerie feeling inside of me watching this film. Not just because the film is about Japanese Americans who were imprisoned during World War II and the communities they built inside the internment camps, but because the main characters in this film, the twins Lane and Lyle, who are both played by actor Aaron Yoo, are based on my great-uncles Lane and Lyle. They are my uncle's father and his father's twin brother portrayed in the film. The film was directed by my uncle's cousin, Desmond Nakano. My uncle's father, Lyle, committed suicide almost 20 years ago. It is strange to watch a young and talented actor such as Aaron Yoo act out your relatives' lives from when they were young men in the internment camps.

Before I viewed *American Pastime* on DVD, I had already begun to schedule interviews with Japanese American women in the Los Angeles area. I was scheduled to interview Kinue, a Japanese American woman, who was the widow of Lyle. The interview was going to take place at her house in Glendale. In September, my own father unexpectedly passed away while on a flight home from Hawaii to Los Angeles on September 11, 2007, a week before my interview with Kinue. It is important to recall there was definitely a presence of sadness surrounding us during our interview, though we did our best to stay focused.

Kinue was born in Lomeda, California, and is a Nisei (second-generation), Japanese American woman. Kinue is part of my extended family. Everyone in my family always speaks of how beautiful and vibrant Kinue is and she is undeniably gorgeous. At 12 years old, she and her family were evacuated to the Heart Mountain internment camp in Wyoming. When she thinks back on the internment camps she says, "The purpose [of the internment camps] to me was horrific. No privacy, I hated the bathrooms, no privacy there." Kinue, called the U.S. Japanese American World War II camps, "concentration camps," which is a term that has been accurately used in literature about the camps. It is understandable to see how a young girl at age 12 would feel self-conscious in a bathroom where there was no privacy.

After she and her family were released from the Heart Mountain internment camp, they moved to Chicago. Kinue says:

> And of course the insecurity . . . I was the only Japanese in the senior [high school] class. I hated it. Hated it, hated it, hated it. I didn't have the tools, the self-esteem or whatever to make friends; I felt very cheated out of my senior year. I do take pride in my parents—I'm getting emotional (starts to cry)—they were quite old. And it's not an option to go on any kind of welfare (crying). They got jobs at dishwashers . . . (starts crying a lot).

> My sister, she had a full scholarship to go to the university but she gave that up because how can you go to college when your family needs help? So she got a job at the same place working in the salad bar. And of course, I took the streetcar and went to school. I was so unhappy! I made myself anorexic. I never ate. I was quite thin and then after that we left to California. My father was college-educated and such with a law degree. And our dream—we were going to college. But with this war and how can we go to school? So coming out here [to California] my sister got a job, I think it was with the city and then eventually I got a job with [the Department of] Water and Power and through friends we borrowed money, my parents borrowed money and bought a duplex. My sister and I gave 50% of our paychecks to our parents to help pay for the little duplex. I don't know how they did it. My father, as old as he was, would go to the Japanese town employment agency and leave on the bus and do housework. My father never lifted a hand at home [before the war] he didn't know how to.

We sat inside of Kinue's beautiful and spacious house in Glendale, California. She collects antiques and has an immaculately clean house. She even baked a whole carrot cake as a present for me to take home. Her house is less than a mile away from the Glendale Community College and she thinks about her education often:

> Of course there are no excuses because Niseis did go to college, working by day and going to school by night. I never did. I guess my biggest regret was the insecurity of never having a college education. I could go now. I could walk to the thing [Glendale Community College], but I'm too lazy. With the discussion in my family, I've always used excuses, saying, "Yeah, I didn't get a college education because of the war." I don't have the motivation to do it. Of course my husband, he was not educated either. He had skills, which you can't get

in school, which are people skills. See, he was the most charismatic person ever and if you were to talk to 10 people they would probably all say that too. But that in turn, became his downfall.

Several years after the internment camps, Kinue and her husband became the owners of a very well-known restaurant in Los Angeles on Sunset Boulevard. This popular restaurant, bar, and nightclub was famous in the '80s. The restaurant was three floors and was in an excellent location. Kinue describes the restaurant:

> See being in that environment, all the celebrities, Frank Sinatra and stuff, Lyle was on a first-name basis with them. That's how he was. They gave him autographs but in that environment he started using drugs and alcohol and I encouraged him to seek help at Betty Ford [rehabilitation center]. And so with the using of drugs, the changing of the whole restaurant climate in L.A., we had customers that used to come every week. His drugs were getting totally out of hand, we were very fortunate to sell [the restaurant]. He sold [it] in 1984. Then in that point in time, I [already] knew in 1982, I would have to get a job and so I did. I knew I was going to have to stand on my feet.

After Kinue and her husband, Lyle, sold the restaurant, Kinue began working at the Los Angeles Great Western Forum nightclub. The Great Western Forum was home to the Los Angeles Lakers basketball team before The Staples Center was built. She never watched a basketball game before nor had she even heard of the Lakers basketball team prior to working at the Forum. Nonetheless, Kinue began working at the nightclub during the mid-80s. Her work and career helped her build self-esteem and kept her life very active. When she talks about her job at the Forum, her face lights up and she says:

> I heard that after I came in, it was the largest generating venue of the private clubs. That made me feel good and I thought, hey, without an education! (Laughs). I managed to . . . well, bottom line for me it managed to boost my self-esteem. They were so good to me and it was so fun. I kind of felt good, but I guess I have to say a lot of women of my generation—relatives—they worked. So with the dysfunction that was going in my family, I've always felt ohhhh . . . well with my husband, 20 years ago he took his life. During that time, I was working. And I went to work two weeks after and to me that was my salvation. You know you have to put your façade, your mask, whatever . . . and it's just like your mom . . . your dad's death. (Starts crying). I can imagine what you guys are going through. With my husband it was by choice, but (crying) finding him . . . it took me one year to feel that Lyle was not going to come through that door. My husband had left a note, he didn't want a funeral. But it does give it closure.

As I have previously mentioned, during the time when I was interviewing some of the Japanese Americans, my own life was overlapping and inter-twining in our discussions. Word spreads quickly in the Japanese American community in Los Angeles, and even if some people did not know my father directly, they knew of his name or his parents name and knew of his passing even if I did not mention it. Though I did not display any visual signs of mourning such as wearing black, I believe some of the women already knew I was mourning which contributed as a catalyst for their own mourning for various past events in their lives. These events and feelings that occurred are all part of the ethnography when discussing the Japanese American community and communication.

Feminist and critical studies research are comprised of locating the relationships found through holistic methods of participant-observation and ethnography in epistemic and natural communities. The interdependence of ethnography, ethics, and theories are important relationships within the realm of naturalized feminist research. Immersing oneself into the culture and entering the lives (when invited) of the women I interviewed brought me, as the ethnographer, into a new relationship with the Japanese American women. The ethnography became a method where the negotiations and connections of accountability, trust, and responsibility were examined, developed, and enacted upon with commitment. Although I had known some of these women for several years or all my life, such as Kinue, my acknowledgement as an outsider to her experiences and knowledge provided her with the power and right to decide how she wanted to share her narrative with me. I had to trust her and her memory, feelings, and perspectives.

Ethnographic research is not without tension and self-inquiry, as it involves ones' physical, mental, and ethical self to participate; she or he becomes vulnerable and responsive to the community she or he is working with to fully engage in the journey of the research. Ethnography is not about the researcher writing about only herself or himself as the subject. Instead, it needs to acknowledge one's location in terms of privilege, race, and power and the gaze or lens from which the experiences are being perceived. Lange (2000) writes, "The world is quite literally perceived and not just interpreted," in a postcolonial framework (p. 229). The importance of ethnography lies in the awareness of the ethnographer to use "the resources, skills, and privileges available to her to make accessible—to penetrate the borders" to reach the voices "otherwise restrained and out of reach" (Madison, 2005, p. 5).

The reflection of self and identity takes place in this ethnographic research on Japanese American women. In the ethnographic study by Reddy (2005), she mentions in the beginning of her book of how she tells her family and friends that she is going to go study hijras and some of them disapprove and that she should not be interacting with them. The communities a researcher inhabits, especially when the community is stigmatized, opens the researcher up to facing the same stigmatization as the community they are researching. I found this to be true. Although I did not face the exact same stigmatization, I was able to relate to the Japanese American women as using silence as a way of coping. My silence was not based upon my experiences in the internment camps, but my own personal challenges of writing about Japanese American women who were similar to me and some of them who were related to me.

Madison (2005) writes the performance of peoples' lives helps to understand their experiences, and all humans perform in ways relating to their identities and communities; this can be said of Japanese American women too. Our identities change and transform due to many factors such as generation, age, regions of where we live, and more. Viewing the performance of Japanese American women who were in the World War II internment camp also made me realize my own performance as a Japanese American woman too. The inquiries of what women reveal and share about themselves, relates to the critical concerns of feminist research made by Butler (2003) about humaneness and the dimensions of how the loss of humanness are enacted upon. Drawing from colonialist perspectives of organized and ideal societies creates perceptions of the Japanese American women's post-internment camp lives as stabilized, which they are not. The on-going feelings and memories of colonization, imprisonment, relocation, and discrimination from World War II, are influenced but not limited to the physical imprisonment and physical liberation from the internment camps. The focus on only physical imprisonment and liberation create a dualistic status that ignores the mental and intergenerational concepts of colonization that can last far beyond the moment when people are liberated from colonization.

Chapter 11

Saying Goodbye and Keeping the Stories Alive

When I finally arrived to the hospital in Santa Barbara, where my grand-mother was in a coma, I was exhausted from traveling. The doctors said she had severe brain and heart damage after her heart attack. My mother and I rented a room on the medical campus and stayed the night with her for a couple of days. In the middle of the night I could not help but wake up crying, feeling as if each muscle strand that held my heart together was unraveling. My heart felt like it was breaking loose with sadness.

The next morning, I woke up and went to my grandmother's hospital bed. The hospital was at a beautiful location and the staff was nice, but it still smelled and felt sterile like a hospital. I was sitting on my grandmother's hospital bed with her, talking to her even though she was in a coma. She hated being alone, especially in a new place. I thought of her as the young girl from Los Angeles, who moved with her mother to Brawley, California, after her father left their family and how she gradually learned to love her step-father, the cantaloupe farmer. She shared experiences with me over and over again about her life in the Poston, Arizona internment camp, such as how after she was released from the internment camp she worked as a domestic servant when she was only 16 years old. She and her family never owned a vacuum cleaner, nor did she know how to use one. She worked for a White family in Michigan. A few months later she was able to move to Chicago. Her parents moved to Chicago before she did so they could find jobs. My grandmother's father obtained a job as a janitor at a bowling company and her mother worked in a sweatshop.

When my grandmother arrived in Chicago as a teenager, her mother got her a job at a sewing factory, selling clothing at "high-end" depart-ment stores where she received a nickel for every dozen shirt collars she sewed. She worked for a few years at the sweatshop factory and she recalls, "And then I had to say to God, 'Here I am, almost 21, if you don't send me a man soon I'm going to have to go back to school. I have to do something else. I can't sew all my life.'" Eventually she and my grandfather met in Chicago. Before he moved to Chicago, he was working in a basket factory in Cleveland, and later he moved to Chicago and worked in a bowling alley. While my grandfather was in Chicago, he was living in a boarding house with 11 other men and was working very hard. My grandmother told me how he used to fall asleep on Chicago's L subway car and wake up and go to work from the subway.

My grandmother and grandfather married, and her parents moved back to Los Angeles. My grandmother's father worked as a gardener. Eventually my grandfather bought a jukebox route, which supplied jukeboxes to the bars in Los Angeles. Throughout time, my grandfather worked very hard and ended up owning a few bars in Los Angeles and gradually sold them throughout the decades as he got older. The last one he sold was when he was 87 years old.

The relocation experiences my grandmother had from Brawley, California, to Poston, Arizona, to Jackson, Michigan, to Chicago, Illinois, and finally back to Los Angeles, California, gave her an extreme distaste for traveling. When she would talk about her internment camp experience, she would follow-up by saying, "That's why I don't like to travel, the stress of all that.

Figure 11.1   A Photo of My Grandparents as Newlyweds After They Were Released from the Internment Camps

It stays with you." Later in her life when she was in her 80s, she began travel-ing with my mother, and loved it. She wanted to travel with her all the time.

I thought of all of this as I sat on the hospital bed next to her. As I held her hand, I felt her fingers stiffen and turn cold. She had passed away as I held her hand and thought of so much of her life that she shared with me. A few minutes later the doctor came into the room and announced she had passed away.

Even though I had faced several challenges during my doctoral degree pro-gram, such as my father passing away and then my grandmother dying, for a few months I could not bare the thought of having to write about the Japanese American women I had interviewed, especially my grandmother. I could not even fathom what it would be like to have to listen to the tape recording of the interview I did with her and transcribe it. The audiotapes sat in a box tucked away into my desk drawer for several weeks.

As time went on, the women I had already interviewed would call me up and tell me they had a friend or family member who was a Japanese American woman and had been in the World War II internment camps, and she was interested in being interviewed for my research project. I could not say no to them. The more women I spoke with, the more I realized how important it is for these stories to stay alive, and they would not stay alive if I kept the audio recordings untouched in a box in my desk. After all the hardships these Japanese American women had faced in the World War II internment camps, and more importantly, their willingness to share part of their lives with me, I realized this was a gift I could not take for granted. If I kept their narratives hidden, I would be contributing to the notorious silence of Japanese American women's lives and histories. Furthermore, I would not only be silencing their stories, I would also be silencing myself as a Japanese American woman because I would also be keeping my story silent. I realized how important it was that I continued to interview, transcribe, and write these narratives in honor of the Japanese American women who shared their lives with me.

KEEPING MEMORIES, HISTORIES, AND NARRATIVES ALIVE

The lives of the Japanese American women who were in the World War II U.S. internment camps were difficult and many of their stories have remained silent. Being seen as an enemy in one's own nation, losing everything they owned, and having to start their lives over again in a country which expressed prejudice and discrimination was a challenge for all the women in this project. Nagata, Trierweiler, and Talbot (1999) found that third-generation Japanese Americans and their communication about their internment camp experiences was often avoided in intergenerational conversations or rarely spoken about to children and grandchildren. Japanese American women who were in the World War II internment camps have had difficulties telling their narratives to their children and grandchildren. Most of the women expressed they have not told their stories or shared very little of their World War II experiences with all their children and grandchildren. I did not want to exclude Japanese American women who did not have children or grandchildren in this book, so I interviewed them too and asked if they had shared their World War II internment camp stories with relatives or friends. Most of them all replied they had not really talked about their experiences but may have mentioned it to a few people. The Japanese American women suggested in their interviews that they have only shared some of their stories with their children or grandchildren when they were asked about it. Though most of the individuals interviewed had not shared their story openly with all the members of their future generations, every individual expressed the importance for not only Japanese Americans, but for all people to know about the World War II internment camps.

Some of the women said they did not share their stories "because they [their children or grandchildren] did not seem interested," does not mean that they view their own stories as insignificant. As Nagata and Cheng (2003) wrote in their research, traumatic events such as the Japanese American internment camps can be communicated intergenerationally through different levels of disclosure and sometimes silence is the only way some individuals cope with the trauma. Some of the women, who have told their stories to their future generations, feel it is important to create awareness about the racism and prejudice they have faced and how they have coped with it (Nagata and Cheng, 2003).

Another interesting topic that revealed itself through the interviews was how several of the women valued the time we shared together discussing their lives. Most of these women who are in their 70s, 80s, and 90s, felt that some of their own families were not interested in their lives or never asked them questions. More than half of the women interviewed are also unmarried or widows and were living alone. A few of the women who I interviewed expressed that it was really nice to have someone come visit them and though we talked about their lives during and after World War II to a great extent, they really seemed excited to have someone to talk and interact with, especially the women who lived alone and had no family nearby. The importance of conversation, interest, and social interaction goes beyond Japanese American women who were in the World War II internment camps, but is also a reminder of how women from all cultural backgrounds can experience loneliness, appreciate social interaction and interest from their loved ones, and value visits from family members and friends.

This project goes beyond the issues and life experiences of Japanese American women; it explores how history, identity, culture, communication, generations, nationality, and power are interwoven in countries around the world including the United States. During World War II there were several other Axis nations besides Japan, such as Germany, Italy, Hungary, Bulgaria, and Romania, but Japanese Americans living on the west coast were specifically targeted and placed in internment camps. The influences of identity and war continue to have affects on many individuals and groups of people living in the United States. The lives of Japanese Americans and the effects of Executive Order 9066 are only a fraction of the inequalities of power and the struggles of race, ethnicity, identity, and culture in the United States.

Issues threatening individuals' identities include the certain states not allowing gay marriage, Arizona's law ordering immigrants to carrying their registration documents (or those who just appear to look like immigrants to be questioned if police or authorities suspect them to be undocumented immigrants), racial violence, and post- 9/11 acts of discrimination against people of Middle Eastern ancestry or of the Muslim religion. The Japanese Americans who have fought for their redress and have shared their stories follow in the civil rights movement of American Indians, African Americans, Latinas/Latinos, Asian Americans, and several groups of people who have fought for equality. There is an ongoing need for awareness, accountability, and responsibility for issues around the world that continue to promote acts of, injustice, violence, and prejudice against people and their identities.

Gandhi's (2004) philosophies on anti-colonial thought focus on how the creation of dualist perspectives striving toward utopian societies often disregard the in-between-ness of other possibilities. The increments of power, stability, economy, and citizenship gained, have the ability to move individuals farther and farther away from their ancestors of their own former identities of otherness (Ong, 1999). The way the Japanese American women in this book have communicated or not communicated their stories does not rely only upon them being Japanese or having a certain amount of Japanese blood running through their veins but the contextualized, historicized, cultural, and socialized negotiations of power, privilege, and politics. The ways in which they have responded to moving beyond focusing on their victimization as colonized individuals should not be interpreted as if the interwar era did not affect them. On the contrary, it affected them with numerous challenges and struggles. Their identities as Americans and the patriotism many of them expressed for their country created identities that do not fit within the postcolonial framework. It was not their choice to be placed in internment camps but many of the Japanese American women and their families made the choice to support the American war efforts through showing their devotion, fighting for their country, and enduring their hardships.

Loyalty

Many of the Japanese American women I interviewed said they did not talk about their World War II experiences to their children or their grandchildren because they suspected they were "not interested" or "they never asked about it." These responses beg further inquiry in future research about the children and grandchildren of the Japanese American women who were interviewed. Perhaps, the children and grandchildren of the Japanese American women interviewed in this research project do know a little bit about their parents and grandparents' experiences but have also chosen silence as a way of coping for themselves, knowing that it is difficult to see their elders mentally relive and talk about their experiences and challenges. Future research suggests we need to inquire, how do we approach our parents and grandparents about discussing their experiences, especially when those experiences are traumatic? The stories and memories of our elders do not last forever. The importance of memories can be the most powerful pathway to our culture's identities, histories, and future.

References

Azuma, E. (2009). Race, citizenship, and the "science of chick sexing": The politics of racial identity among Japanese Americans. *Pacific Historical Review, 78,* 242–275.

Ball, H. (2001). Judicial parsimony and military necessity disinterred: A reexamination of the Japanese exclusion cases, 1943–1944. In R. Daniels, S.C. Taylor, & H.L. Kitano (Eds.), *Japanese Americans: From relocation to redress* (pp. 176–185). Seattle: University of Washington Press.

Barnlund, D. (1975). *Public and private self in Japan and the United States.* Tokyo: Simul.

Barocas, H.A. (1971). A note on the children of concentration camp survivors. *Psychotherapy Patient, 8,* 189–190.

Bishop, R. (2000). To protect and serve: The "guard dog" function of journalism in coverage of the Japanese-American internment. *Journalism and Communication Monographs, 2,* 65–95.

Butler, J. (2004). *Undoing gender.* New York, NY: Routledge.

Constantine, M.G. (2007). Racial microaggressions against African American clients in a cross-racial counseling relationship. *Journal of Counseling Psychology, 54,* 1–16.

Cook, E.P. (1990). Gender and psychological distress. *Journal of Counseling and Development, 68,* 371–375.

Creighton, M. (1997). Whispered silences: Japanese Americans and World War II. *Pacific Affairs, 70,* 637–639.

Daniels, R. (2002). Incarcerating Japanese Americans. *Magazine of History, 16,* 19–24.

Daniels, R., & Kitano, H. (1970). *American racism.* Englewood Cliffs, NJ: Prentice Hall.

Daniels, R., Taylor, S.T., & Kitano, H.H.L. (Eds.). (1986). *Japanese Americans: From relocation to redress.* Seattle, WA: University of Washington Press.

Donohue, G.A., Tichenor, P.J., & Olien, C.N. (1995). A guard dog perspective on the role of media. *Journal of Communication, 45(2),* 115–132.

Ethier, K., & Deaux, K. (1994). Negotiating social identity when contexts change: Maintaining identification and responding to threat. *Journal of Personality and Social Psychology, 67,* 243–251.

Foucault, M. (1984). Truth and power. In P. Rabinow (Ed.), *The Foucault reader* (pp. 51–75). New York: Pantheon Books.

Foucault, M. (1984). The body of the condemned. In P. Rabinow (Ed.), *The Foucault reader* (pp. 171–178). New York: Pantheon Books.

Gandhi, L. (2006). *Affective communities: Anticolonial thought, Fin-De-Siecle radicalism, and the politics of friendship.* Durham: Duke University Press.

Gardiner, C.H. (2001). The Latin-American Japanese and World War II. In R. Daniels, S.C. Taylor, & H.H.L. Kitano (Eds.), *Japanese Americans: From relocation to redress* (pp. 142–145). Seattle: University of Washington Press.

Goldstein, B.Z., & Tamure, K. (1975). *Japan and America: A comparative study in language and culture.* Rutland, VT: Charles E. Tuttle.

Gudykunst, W.B. (2001). *Asian American ethnicity and communication.* Thousand Oaks, CA: Sage.

Gudykunst, W.B., Gao, G., Nishida, T., Nadamitsu, Y., & Sakai, J. (1992). Self-monitoring in Japan and the United States. In S. Iwawaki, Y. Kashima, & K. Leung (Eds.), *Innovations in cross-cultural psychology* (pp. 185–198). Lisse, the Netherlands: Swets & Zeitlinger.

Gudykunst, W.B. Matsumoto, Y., Ting-Toomey, S., Nishida, T., Kim, K., & Heyman, S. (1996). The influence of cultural individualism-collectivism, self construals, and individual values on communication styles across cultures. *Human Communication Research, 12,* 525–549.

Gudykunst, W.B., & Ting-Toomey, S. (1988). *Culture, and interpersonal communication.* Newbury Park, CA: Sage.

Gudykunst, W.B., Yoon, Y.C., & Nishida, T. (1987). The influence of individualism-collectivism on perceptions of communication in ingroup-outgroup relationships. *Communication Monographs, 54,* 293–306.

Hall, E.T. (1976). *Beyond culture.* New York, NY: Doubleday.

Halualani, R.T. (2002). *In the name of Hawaiians: Native identities and cultural politics.* Minneapolis: University of Minnesota Press.

Hecht, M.L., & Baldwin, J.R. (1998). Layers and holograms: A new look at prejudice. In M.L. Hecht (Ed.), *Communicating prejudice.* Thousand Oaks, CA: Sage Publications.

Heider, K.G. (1976). *Ethnographic film.* Austin: University of Texas Press.

Higashide, S., Gardiner, C.H., & Kudo, E.H. (2000). *Adios to tears: The memoirs of a Japanese-Peruvian internee in U.S. concentration camps.* Seattle, WA: University of Seattle Press.

Hohri, W. (2001). Redress as a movement towards enfranchisement. In R. Daniels, S.C. Taylor, & H.L. Kitano (Eds.), *Japanese Americans: From relocation to redress* (pp. 196–199). Seattle: University of Washington Press.

Hirasuna, D. (2005). *The art of gaman: Arts and crafts from Japanese American internment camps 1942–1946.* Berkeley, CA: Ten Speed Press.

Hofstede, G. (1979). Value systems in forty countries. In L. Eckenberger, W. Lonner, & Y. Poortinga (Eds.), *Cross-cultural contributions in psychology* (pp. 389–407). Amsterdam: Swets and Zeitlinger.

Inada, L.F. (Ed.). (2000). *Only what we could carry.* San Francisco, CA: Heyday Books.

Ishizawa, H. (2004). Minority language use among grandchildren in multigenerational households. *Social Perspectives, 47,* 465–483.

Ivey, A.E., & Ivey, M.B. (1999). *Intentional interviewing and counseling* (4th ed.). Pacific Grove, CA: Brooks Cole.

Iwamura, J.N. (2007). Critical faith: Japanese Americans and the birth of a new civil religion. *American Quarterly, 59,* 937–968.

Kim, U. (1994). Individualism and collectivism: Conceptual clarification and elaboration. In U. Kim, H. Triandis, C. Kagitcibasi, S.-C. Choi, & G. Yoon (Eds.), *Individualism and collectivism: Theory, method, and applications* (pp. 19–40). Thousand Oaks, CA: Sage.

Kim, Y. (1998). *Communication and cross-cultural adaptation: An integrative theory.* Clevedon, UK: Multilingual Matters.

Koening, W. (1964). Chronic or persisting identity diffusion. *American Journal of Psychiatry, 120,* 1081–1084.

Kramer, E.M. (2003). *The emerging monoculture: Assimilation and the "Model Minority."* Westport, CT: Praeger.

Krishnaswamy, R. (2008). Postcolonial and global studies: Connections, conflicts, complicities. In R. Krishnaswamy & J.C. Hawley (Eds.), *The post-colonial and the global.* Minneapolis: University of Minnesota Press.

Krishnaswamy, R., & Hawley, J.C. (Eds.). (2008). *The post-colonial and the global.* Minneapolis: University of Minnesota Press.

Lange, L. (2000). Burnt offerings to rationality: A feminist reading of the contruction of indigenous peoples in Enrique Dussels theory of modernity. In U. Narayan & S. Harding (Eds.), *Decentering the center* (pp. 226–239). Bloomington, IN: Indiana University Press.

Lee, R. (1999). *Orientals: Asian Americans in popular culture.* Philadelphia: Temple University Press.

Lim, T. (2002). Language and verbal communication across cultures. In W.B. Gudykunst & B. Mody (Eds.), *Handbook of international and intercultural communication.* Thousand Oaks, CA: Sage.

Lindloff, T., & Taylor, B. (2002). *Qualitative communication research methods* (2nd ed.). Thousand Oaks: Sage.

Lu, X. (2001). Bicultural identity development and Chinese community formation: An ethnographic study of Chinese schools in Chicago. *The Howard Journal of Communications, 12,* 203–220.

Luther, C.A. (2003). Reflections of cultural identities in conflict: Japanese American internment camp newspapers during World War II. *Journal History, 29,* 69–83.

Madison, D.S. (2005). *Critical ethnography: Method ethics, and performance.* Thousand Oaks, CA: Sage Publications.

Matsumoto, V. (2000). Japanese American women during World War II. In V.L. Ruiz & E.C. Dubois (Eds.), *Unequal sisters: A multicultural reader in U.S. women's history* (3rd ed.). (pp. 478–491). New York: Routeledge.

Mizutani, O., & Mizutani, N. (1987). *How to be polite in Japanese.* Tokyo: Japan Times.

Molina, N. (2006). Inverting racial logic: How public health discourse and standards racialized the meanings of Japanese and Mexican in Los Angeles, 1910–1924. In N. De Genova (Ed.), *Racial transformations* (pp. 40–62). Durham: Duke University Press.

Morsbach, H. (1976). Aspects of nonverbal communication in Japan. In L. Samovar & R. Porter (Eds.), *Intercultural communication: A reader* (2nd ed.). Belmont, CA: Wadsworth.

Mosher, J. (2002). By order of the president: FDR and the internment of Japanese Americans. *Perspectives on Political Science, 31,* 189.

Nagata, D.K., Trierweiler, S.J., & Talbot, R. (1999). Long-term effects of internment during early childhood on third-generation Japanese Americans. *American Journal of Orthopsychiatry, 69,* 19–29.

Nagata, D.K., & Cheng, W. (2003). Intergeneration communication of race-related trauma by Japanese American former internees. *American Journal of Orthopsychiatry, 73,* 266–278.

Okihiro, G.Y. (1994). *Margins and mainstreams: Asians in American history and culture.* Seattle, WA: University of Washington Press.

Ong, A. (1999). *Flexible citizenship: The cultural logics of transnationality.* Durham: Duke University Press.

Ono, K. (Ed.). (2005). *Asian American studies after critical mass.* Malden, MA: Blackwell Publishing.

Orbe, M.P., & Harris, T.M. (2008). *Interracial communication* (2nd ed.). Los Angeles: Sage.

Phu, T. (2008). The spaces of human confinement: Manzanar photography and landscape ideology. *Journal of Asian American Studies, 11,* 337–371.

Pollak, R. (2004). An intergenerational model of domestic-violence. *Journal of Population Economics, 17,* 311–329.

Rabinow, P. (Ed.). (1984). *The Foucault reader.* New York: Pantheon Books.

Rantanen, T. (2002). *Theorizing media and globalization.* Thousand Oaks, CA: Sage.

Reddy, G. (2005). *With respect to sex.* Chicago: The University of Chicago Press.

Rogers, E.M, & Hart, W.B. (2002). The histories of intercultural, international, and development communication. In W.B. Gudykunst & B. Moody (Eds.), *International and intercultural communication* (2nd ed.). (pp. 1–18). Thousand Oaks, CA: Sage.

Ruiz, V.L., & DuBois, E.C. (Eds.). (2000). *Unequal sisters: A multicultural reader in U.S. women's history* (3rd ed.). New York: Routeledge.

Schmoe, F. (2001). Seattle's peace churches and relocation. In R. Daniels, S.C. Taylor, & H.L. Kitano (Eds.), *Japanese Americans: From relocation to redress* (117–122). Seattle: University of Washington Press.

Schvaneveldt, P., Kerpelman, J., & Schvaneveldt, D. (2005). Generational and cultural changes in family life in the United Arab Emirates: A comparison of mothers and daughters. *Journal of Comparative Family Studies, 36,* 77–91.

Shome, R. (1999). Whiteness and the politics of location: Postcolonial reflections. In T.K. Nakayama & J.N. Martin (Eds.), *Whiteness: The communication of social identity*. Thousand Oaks, CA: Sage Publications.

Solkoff, N. (1981). Children of survivors of the Nazi Holocaust: A critical review of the literature. *American Journal of Orthopsychiatry, 51,* 29–42.

Sone, M. (1995). *Nisei daughter*. Seattle, WA: University of Seattle Press.

Spradley, J.P. (1979). *The ethnographic interview*. New York: Holt, Rinehart, and Winston.

Sue, D.W. Capodilupo, C.M., Nadal, K.L., & Torino, G.C. (2008). Racial microaggressions and the power to define reality. *American Psychologist, 62,* 271–286.

Sue, D.W., & Sue, D. (2008). *Counseling the culturally diverse: Theory and practice* (5th ed.). New York: Wiley.

Tamura, T., & Lau, A. (1992). Connectedness versus separateness: Applicability of family-therapy to Japanese families. *Family Process, 31,* 319–340.

Tateishi, J. (2001). The Japanese American Citizens League and the struggle for redress. In R. Daniels, S.C. Taylor, & H.H.L. Kitano (Eds.), *Japanese Americans: From relocation to redress* (pp. 191–195). Seattle: University of Washington Press.

Ting-Toomey, S. (1999). *Communicating across cultures*. New York, NY: Guilford.

Tohe, L. (1998). A contextual statement surrounding three poems of prejudice. In M.L. Hecht (Ed.), *Communicating prejudice* (pp. 246–256). Thousand Oaks, CA: Sage Publications.

Uba, L. (1994). *Asian Americans*. New York: Guilford.

Uno, K. (2000). Pearl Harbor remembers. In L.W. Inada (Ed.), *Only what we could carry* (pp. 31–32). Berkeley, CA: Heyday Books.

Weiss, E., O'Connell, A.N., & Siiter, R. (1986). Comparisons of second-generation Holocaust survivors, immigrants, and nonimmigrants on measures of mental health. *Journal of Personality and Social Psychology, 50,* 828–831.

Yamaguchi, S. (1994). Collectivism among the Japanese: A perspective from the self. In U. Kim, H. Triandis, C. Kagitcibasi, S.-C. Choi, & G. Yoon (Eds.), *Individualism and collectivism: Theory, method, and applications* (pp. 175–188). Thousand Oaks, CA: Sage.

Yin, R. (2003). *Case study: Design and methods*. Thousand Oaks, CA: Sage Publications.

Young, M. (2004). *Minor re/visions. Asian American literacy narratives as a rhetoric of citizenship*. Carbondale, IL: Southern Illinois University Press.

Yuki, M., & Brewer, M.B. (1999, August). *Japanese collectivism versus American collectivism: A comparison of group-loyalty across the cultures*. Paper presented at the Asian Social Psychology Association conference, Taipei.

Zia, H. (2000). *Asian American dreams: The emergence of an American people*. New York: Farrar, Straus and Giroux.

Index

About the Author

Precious Yamaguchi, Ph.D. is an assistant professor of communication at Southern Oregon University in Ashland, Oregon.